IGCSE
First Language English

Second edition
Marian Cox

CAMBRIDGE
UNIVERSITY PRESS

To Robert, for his technical, intellectual and emotional support

CAMBRIDGE UNIVERSITY PRESS
Cambridge, New York, Melbourne, Madrid, Cape Town, Singapore, São Paulo

Cambridge University Press
The Edinburgh Building, Cambridge CB2 8RU, UK

www.cambridge.org
Information on this title: www.cambridge.org/9780521693066

First published 2002
Second edition 2006
Reprinted 2007

Printed in the United Kingdom at the University Press, Cambridge

A catalogue record for this publication is available from the British Library

ISBN 978-0-521-69306-6 paperback

Cover image © Royalty-Free/Corbis

Illustrations by Peter and Janet Simmonett, and Kate Charlesworth

Picture research by Sara Payne

Contents

Introduction to the second edition   *v*

Objectives of the examination   *vii*

Components of the examination   *vii*

Part 1 Leisure: sport, travel, pastimes

Unit 1: *Reading: skimming and scanning, selecting points for summary, making notes using your own words, looking at writers' language choices*   *1*

Unit 2: *Directed writing: diaries, formal and informal letters, considering audience, choosing a style*   *9*

Unit 3: *Composition: planning continuous writing, descriptive compositions, using adjectives and imagery*   *18*

Unit 4: *Speaking and listening: preparing a talk, conversation skills*   *28*

Part 2 Work: information, education, employment

Unit 5: *Reading: understanding, selecting and organising material for summary questions*   *36*

Unit 6: *Directed writing: presenting and transforming information, news reports, formal reports*   *46*

Unit 7: *Composition: giving an account, organising information chronologically*   *56*

Unit 8: *Speaking and listening: role-play dialogues, preparing an interview*   *64*

Part 3 People: society, lifestyles, relationships

Unit 9: *Reading: expanding notes, sentence structure, vocabulary building, summary style, collating texts, how writers achieve effects*   *73*

Unit 10: *Directed writing: persuasive writing, analysing techniques, writing publicity material, drawing inferences, writing in role, targeting an audience*   *84*

Unit 11: *Composition: composing narratives, engaging the reader, dialogue punctuation*   *95*

Unit 12: *Speaking and listening: paired and group discussion, facts and opinions*   *105*

Part 4 Ideas: art, science, technology

Unit 13: *Reading: collating texts, analysing style, vocabulary building, advanced punctuation*   *114*

Unit 14: *Directed writing: expressing and supporting a view, collating and ordering information, reports and articles*   *124*

Unit 15: *Composition: making a case, constructing an argument, presenting a discussion, using rhetorical devices, improving spelling*   *133*

Unit 16: *Speaking and listening: defending opinions, delivering a speech*   *142*

List of terms   *150*

Acknowledgements   *151*

Introduction to the second edition

The International General Certificate of Secondary Education (IGCSE) First Language English syllabus is designed as a two-year course for examination at age 16+ for students whose English is of native, near-native or bilingual standard. It was introduced in 1986 to offer a wide, relevant and accessible curriculum tailored to international needs and a fair assessment scheme which rewards positive achievement rather than penalising errors. First Language English is accepted as a UK higher education entrance requirement equivalent to British GCSE or IELTS 6.5, and is recognised as a suitable foundation for A level and IB studies.

This coursebook covers the whole IGCSE First Language curriculum and contains enough material for the two-year programme of study. The syllabus underwent revision in 2005 and this book prepares candidates for the revised syllabus. Each of the 16 units has a rich variety of activities and tasks sufficient to last for several classroom lessons plus homework. Teachers may wish to be selective in order to target the particular needs of their students. Each unit ends with three further practice tasks for students to do at home. It would be possible for students to use the coursebook without a teacher as the frequent exam tips give support, explication and, in many cases, answers to the questions and tasks. All the experience and advice needed for students to perform at the highest level in the examination is provided and reinforced.

You are advised to work through the units in sequence as the learning guidance and skills development are progressive. Although there is specific teaching of sentence building, vocabulary extension, punctuation and spelling, the book is intended primarily for use as an exam preparation course rather than as a language coursebook. The emphasis is therefore on the acquisition and application of transferable skills, with a mixture of preparatory and exam-type tasks in every unit. A complementary student workbook is available, in the same series and by the same author, which not only gives support and practice, but also contains further exam-type passages and tasks, as well as composition and coursework titles. Advice in the exam tips is based on University of Cambridge International Examinations (CIE) documents relating to the exam. Question papers and the mark scheme for the IGCSE First Language English examination are available from CIE and on the CIE website www.cie.org.uk.

The coursebook focuses on Paper 2 but it is also suitable for Paper 1 (Reading Passage(s)) since the components have a reading text in common and there is an overlap of skills assessed between the core and extended levels. Although Paper 3 is the focus of the book's practice in Directed Writing and Composition, there is much advice on types of writing, content, structure and style which would be equally applicable to coursework portfolio pieces, and there are suggestions for possible coursework assignment topics and provision of a variety of stimulus resources in each Composition unit.

The IGCSE First Language Speaking and Listening component – though an optional part of the exam – is more than adequately covered in the book, with numerous opportunities for skills acquisition and classroom practice in a variety of groupings and situations which prepare students for both Paper 5 and Paper 6. Four units concentrate on speaking and listening, and in addition every unit contains aural and oral communication activities. This is consistent with an integrated-skills approach to the teaching and learning of language and an interactive and investigative classroom methodology in line with the good practice implied in the aims of IGCSE.

The book is divided into four themed sections: Leisure, Work, People and Ideas. Each section is sub-divided into units corresponding to the four exam assessment areas: Reading, Directed writing, Composition, and Speaking and listening. The themes were chosen for their international applicability, relevance, variety and intrinsic interest to young people. The majority of texts are authentic and recent; they are also typical of the kinds of passages and tasks set by the exam board. Furthermore, the book draws upon a wide variety of sources, genres, registers and issues, and has been designed to be user friendly as well as academically stimulating. Quotations included in the exam-tip boxes are taken from the IGCSE First Language English syllabus.

Students are expected to have a good-quality dictionary available, and to keep a record of new vocabulary in a personal list as they work through the book. A thesaurus may also be useful, if used sensibly. They will need some different-coloured highlighters and/or pens for selecting material from passages, and an exercise book or supply of file paper.

By the end of the coursebook students should have become more confident in thinking about language, handling and responding to texts, and approaching and fulfilling tasks. They should also have expanded their vocabulary, increased their accuracy, and improved in all the skills areas so that they are fully prepared to sit the exam.

Objectives of the examination

Reading Objectives:
R1   Understand and collate explicit meanings
R2   Understand, explain and collate implicit meanings and attitudes
R3   Select, analyse and evaluate what is relevant to specific purposes
R4   Understand how writers achieve effects

Writing Objectives:
W1   Articulate experiences and express what is thought, felt and imagined
W2   Order and present facts, ideas and opinions
W3   Understand and use a range of appropriate vocabulary
W4   Use language and register appropriate to audience and context
W5   Make accurate and effective use of paragraphs, grammatical structures, sentences, punctuation and spelling

Speaking Objectives:
S1   Understand, order and present facts, ideas and opinions
S2   Articulate experience and express what is thought, felt and imagined
S3   Communicate clearly and fluently
S4   Use language and register appropriate to audience and context
S5   Listen to and respond appropriately to the contributions of others

Components of the examination

Component 1: Reading Passage (Core) (1 hour 45 minutes)
Questions will relate to one passage of approximately 700–800 words that is printed on the question paper.

Question 1 (30 marks) will be divided into a series of sub-questions requiring answers of different lengths. These will be based on the passage provided on the question paper. It will test the following Reading Objectives: R1–R4.

Question 2 (20 marks) will require candidates to respond to the passage printed on the question paper. It will test the following Reading Objectives (10 marks): R1–R3. In addition, 10 marks will be available for Writing Objectives W1–W5.

Component 2: Reading Passage (Extended) (2 hours)
Questions will relate to two passages of approximately 600–700 words each, linked by a common theme. These passages will be printed on the question paper.

Question 1 (20 marks), which may be sub-divided, will require candidates to respond to Passage 1 only. It will test the following Reading Objectives (15 marks): R1–R3. In addition, 5 marks will be available for Writing Objectives W1–W5.

Question 2 (10 marks), which may be sub-divided, will be based on Passage 1 only. It will test Reading Objective R4.

Question 3 (20 marks), which may be sub-divided, will require candidates to write a summary based on Passage 1 *and* Passage 2. It will test the following Reading Objectives (15 marks): R1–R3. In addition, 5 marks will be available for Writing Objectives W1–W5.

Component 3: Directed Writing & Composition (both Core & Extended) (2 hours)

Section 1 – Directed Writing (25 marks)

Candidates will read one or more short texts, which will be printed on the question paper. They will be required to use and develop the given information in another form, e.g. a letter, a report, a speech, a dialogue of about 250–300 words. The question will test the following Writing Objectives (15 marks): W1–W5. In addition, 10 marks will be available for Reading Objectives R1–R3.

Section 2 – Composition (25 marks)

Two argumentative/discursive, two descriptive and two narrative titles will be set. Candidates will be required to write on one title only. Candidates will be advised to write between 350 and 450 words. This section will test the following Writing Objectives: W1–W5.

Component 4: Coursework Portfolio (both Core & Extended)

Candidates will be required to submit a portfolio of **three** assignments, each of about 500–800 words. These assignments may be done in any order. The final mark for the Coursework Portfolio will be out of 50.

Assignment 1: informative, analytical and/or argumentative

Assignment 2: imaginative, descriptive and/or narrative

Assignment 3: a response to a text or texts chosen by the Centre. The text(s) should contain facts, opinions and arguments. Candidates will be required to respond to the text(s) by selecting, analysing and evaluating points from the material (Reading Objectives R1–R3). They may write in any appropriate form they wish.

The Coursework Portfolio will test the following Writing Objectives (40 marks): W1–W5. For Assignment 3 only, an additional 10 marks will be available for Reading Objectives R1–R3. Candidates must include the first draft for **one** of the three assignments submitted.

Component 5: Speaking & Listening (Optional)

There will be two parts to the test:

Part 1 – Individual Task (3–4 minutes) (10 marks)

For example, a presentation, a talk, a speech, a monologue. The candidate will talk for about 3–4 minutes on a single topic or theme which has been selected by her/him prior to the test. The Individual Task will test the following Speaking Objectives: S1–S4.

Part 2 – Discussion (6–7 minutes) (20 marks)

The Individual Task will lead into a conversation with the teacher/examiner about the candidate's chosen topic. The Discussion will test the following Speaking Objectives: S1–S5.

Component 6: Speaking & Listening Coursework (Optional)

Candidates will be assessed on their performance during the course in three different speaking and listening tasks:

Task 1: an individual activity

Task 2: a pair-based activity

Task 3: a group activity

Tasks will be equally weighted in the final assessment and will test the following Speaking Objectives: S1–S5 (S5 for Tasks 2 and 3 only).

Part 1

Leisure: sport, travel, pastimes

Unit 1: *Reading*

This unit focuses on reading for gist and for specific information, and on the selection of key points for summary and on writers' choice of language.

1 You are going to read a passage about an island. To get you in the mood, with your partner jot down words associated with *islands*. Create a **spider diagram**, with *islands* as the central 'body' and associated ideas (e.g. *tropical, remote, coconuts*) as the 'legs'.

2 Looking at your spider diagram, think about possible answers to the following questions:

a   Which islands or types of island are you imagining?
b   Why are islands generally considered attractive?
c   What are the disadvantages of living on or being on an island?

3 Skim read the passage on page 2, written by a travel writer about the island of Corsica.

4 Without looking at the passage, answer the following general questions. Compare your answers with your partner's.

a   What is the most noticeable feature of the scenery?
b   Where can tourists spend their time?
c   What is the main means of transport?
d   What is the basis of the Corsican economy?
e   How do the locals appear to visitors?

> **▼ Exam tip!**   *relates to Exercises 3, 4 and 5*
>
> Time is allowed for you to read exam texts twice. First, **skim** the text to get the **gist** (the main ideas and features). Second, **scan** for specific information to answer the question. You are expected to spend 15 minutes reading the two passages of 600–700 words each, linked by a common theme, on Paper 2. The first passage may be from a literary text. You are advised to answer questions 1 and 2 before reading the second passage, which relates to question 3 only.

A circuit of Corsica

Corsica is France, but it is not French. It is a mountain range moored like a great ship with a cargo of crags a hundred miles off the Riviera. In its three climates it combines the high Alps, the ruggedness of North Africa, and the choicest landscapes of Italy, but most dramatic are the peaks, which are never out of view and show in the upheaval of rock a culture that is violent and heroic. The landscape is just weird enough to be beautiful and too large to be pretty. On the west are cliffs which drop straight and red into the sea; on the south there is a true fjord; on the east a long, flat, and formerly malarial coast with the island's only straight road; on the north a populous cape; and in the centre the Gothic steeples of mountains, fringed by forests where wild boar are hunted.

There are sandy beaches, pebbly beaches, boulder-strewn beaches; beaches with enormous waves breaking over them and beaches that are little more than mud flats; beaches with hotels and beaches that have never known the taint of a tourist's footprint. There are five-star hotels and hotels that are unfit for human habitation.

A car seems a necessity, but cars are easy to hire, and, driving, one discovers how small Corsica is, how much can be seen in a week. All the roads are dangerous; many are simply the last mile to an early grave. 'There are no bad drivers in Corsica,' a Corsican told me. 'All the bad drivers die very quickly.' But he was wrong – I saw many and I still have damp palms to prove it. I had decided to make a circuit of Corsica, to rent a car and drive slowly around the edge of the island, then pause and make my way over the mountains, from Moriani-Plage via Corte to Île Rousse, arriving where I had begun, in Ajaccio, the capital city.

Two decades ago the island was dying economically, but the arrival of ex-colonials from Algeria brought mechanised wine-making methods and the growing of mandarin oranges to Corsica. And now there is a degree of prosperity in Corsica's agriculture, with the export of cheap wine. The good wine – and it is not the plonk the mainlanders say it is – is drunk locally. The Corsican table wine that is exported is little more than red ink.

The Corsicans have a reputation for being unfriendly. They certainly look gloomy, and their character is incontestably sullen; but they are not smug or critical, they can be helpful, and they seem genuinely interested in strangers. 'Simple in manner and thoroughly obliging,' wrote the English poet Edward Lear, 'anxious to please the traveller, yet free from compliment and servility.' One old woman in the market at Île Rousse told me in pidgin Italian that she thought Americans were 'sweet'. It is not a sentiment I have heard expressed anywhere else in Europe.

Source: Adapted from Paul Theroux, 'A circuit of Corsica', *Atlantic Monthly,* November 1978

5 Now scan the passage and highlight the single word in each paragraph which could be used as a heading for that paragraph. Are your choices the same as your partner's?

▼ *Exam tip!*

A summary is a reduced version of a text and its aim is informative. When you write a summary of a passage, you need to identify the key words in the text (single words or phrases which tell you what each part of the text is about). It is useful to have two highlighters, in different colours, with you in the exam so that you can select different kinds of summary material for the two-part question.

6 Skim read the passage below and divide it into paragraphs as you read, using this symbol: //

Cape Town

With its majestic Table Mountain backdrop, Cape Town is one of the most beautiful cities in the world. A harmonious blend of architectural styles reflects the tastes of the past as well as today's more functional requirements. Between the high-rise office blocks, Edwardian and Victorian buildings have been meticulously preserved, and many outstanding examples of Cape Dutch architecture are found. Narrow, cobblestone streets and the strongly Islamic presence of the Bo-Kaap enhance the cosmopolitan ambiance of the city.//Cape Town's shopping options invite you to endlessly browse. Elegant malls such as the Victoria Wharf at the V & A Waterfront, antique shops, craft markets, flea markets and art galleries abound. Specialist boutiques offer an enticing array of unusual items not readily obtainable elsewhere.//One of Cape Town's biggest tourist attractions, the Waterfront, evokes images of the early activities of the harbour. Much of its charm lies in the fact that this busy commercial harbour is set in the midst of a huge entertainment venue with pubs, restaurants, shops, craft markets, theatres and movies.//Table Mountain is undeniably the biggest tourist attraction in South Africa, drawing local holidaymakers as well as tourists from the four corners of the globe. The summit can be reached by trails or cable-car, but mountaineers do it the hard way. On a clear day, the spectacular views from the summit (1,086 metres above sea level) stretch across the mountainous spine of the Cape Peninsula and beyond Table Bay and Robben Island.//Robben Island, which lies about 11 kilometres north of Cape Town, has over the years become synonymous with the anti-apartheid struggle in South Africa. It was here that activists like Nelson Mandela and Walter Sisulu, among many others, were imprisoned because of their opposition to apartheid. The historical importance of Robben Island (meaning 'Seal Island') can be gauged by its designation as a cultural heritage site.//Stretching away from Table Bay Harbour, the Atlantic seafront features virgin beaches along undeveloped frontages to the north, and densely populated Sea Point to the south, leading on to the Clifton, Camps Bay and Llandudno beauty spots, among others. The western coastline is characterised by rocky outcrops and beautiful beaches. Major national and international windsurfing competitions are held at Bloubergstrand. Seal watching is an amusing diversion. Boat trips around the harbour and along the coast are always popular.

Source: Adapted from http://www.sa-venues.com

▼ *Exam tip!*

A paragraph is a logical way of dividing text into topic areas. Paragraphs group similar information together, and a break between paragraphs shows a change of idea, time or place. As well as being necessary for structuring text, paragraphs are a courtesy to the reader.

---

7 How many paragraphs did you make? Compare and discuss with your partner why you put breaks where you did.

8 Scan the passage and, in the margin, give each of the paragraphs a heading to indicate its topic, as if for a tourist brochure. This time, instead of using words from the passage, try to think of **synonyms** (words or phrases with the same meaning).

Exam tip! See next page ▶

▼ *Exam tip!* relates to Exercise 8

If you are asked to respond in your own words, be careful to avoid 'lifting' from the text – i.e. copying whole phrases or sentences. 'Lifting' is penalised in the writing marks for questions 1 and 3 on Paper 2.

9 **Summarise** in one sentence the attractions Cape Town has for visitors, according to the passage.

▼ *Exam tip!*

It is good style, saves time and words, and avoids repetition to use complex sentences when writing English. A **complex sentence** has at least two clauses (groups of words containing finite verbs): one **main clause**, which could stand as a sentence on its own, and one or more **subordinate clauses**, which are not grammatically complete as sentences on their own and should be separated from the main clause by commas. Subordinate clauses are usually introduced by **connectives**. There is an example of a complex sentence at the end of the following text.

10 Read the following passage about a stop in Egypt during a journey from the North Pole to the South Pole without using air transport.

Day 56 – Luxor

At 5.35 in the morning the train pulls into Luxor, known by the Greeks as Thebes, 420 miles south of Cairo, in Upper Egypt. I cannot conceal my excitement at being here for the first time in my life.

Luxor Station is tastefully <u>monumental</u> in decoration, with tall columns, gilded details on the doors, eagle heads and a <u>hieroglyphic</u> design somehow <u>incorporating</u> power stations, railways and ancient history. Figures materialise from the pre-dawn gloom to offer us taxi rides. You will never stand on your own for long in Egypt.

We shall be joining a Nile cruise for the next leg of our journey, and as we drive along the river to find our boat – the Isis – I can see ranks of chunky four-storeyed vessels, maybe 100 in all, lined up along the riverbank, awaiting the day the tourists come back.

My guide to Luxor is a tall, straight, matchstick-thin aristocrat of the business whose name is Tadorus but who asks me to call him Peter … 'It's easier.' I would rather call him Tadorus, but he doesn't look the sort you argue with. He is 83 years old, and as a boy of 14 was present when the <u>archaeologist</u> Howard Carter first pushed open the door of Tutankhamun's tomb.

Peter takes me across on the Nile ferry to a cluster of mud buildings on the West Bank opposite the city. We are driven past fields of sugar cane and alongside an irrigation canal financed by the Russians in 1960. The greenery ends abruptly as we climb a winding road up into barren, rubble-strewn desert. Then we are into the Valley of the Kings, which resembles a gigantic quarry, littered with rock <u>debris</u>, bleached white by the sun. We leave the bus and walk up towards the tombs in dry and scorching heat. Peter estimates the temperature at 40° Celsius, 104° Fahrenheit.

This vast necropolis contains the remains of 62 Pharaohs of the New Kingdom, established in Thebes 3,000 to 3,500 years ago. It was discovered – 'rediscovered,' as Peter corrects me – in 1892. Only 40 of the tombs have been found, and all, bar one, had been emptied by robbers.

We walk down into the tomb of Rameses III. The walls are covered in rich paintings and complex inscriptions illustrating the progress of the Pharaoh on his journey through the underworld, filled with wicked serpents, crocodiles and other creatures waiting to <u>devour</u> him. Because of the dry desert air, they are well preserved, an extraordinary historical document.

The sun is setting behind the Valley of the Kings when we return on the ferry. At this indescribably beautiful time of day, when the rich golden brown of the lower sky spills onto the surface of the Nile, turning it an intense amber, and the palm trees along the bank glow for a few precious minutes in the reflection, it is not difficult to imagine the power and spectacle of a funeral procession bearing the God-King's body across this same river, three and a half thousand years ago, at the beginning of his last and most important journey.

Source: Adapted from Michael Palin, *Pole to Pole*, BBC Publishing, London, 1995

11 Six words in the passage are underlined. Can you guess their meaning by looking at their **context** (the other words around them)? Use a dictionary to check your guesses and write synonyms for the six words in your personal vocabulary list.

> ▼ *Exam tip!*
>
> Don't worry about a few unfamiliar words in an exam text. You can often guess a word's meaning from its context or by recognising part of the word or its prefix. In any case, you may not need to understand every word in a text to write a summary of the parts of it which are specified in the question. Nevertheless, it is useful exam preparation to keep a personal vocabulary list during the course. Writing down words helps you to remember them and to use them in your own writing.

12 Which words and phrases in the passage best illustrate the appearance of

    a the West Bank and the Valley of the Kings (paragraph 5)?
    b the tomb of Rameses III (paragraph 7)?
    c the Nile at sunset (paragraph 8)?

For each of your choices, explain their effectiveness.

> ▼ *Exam tip!*
>
> Paper 2 question 2 requires you to select and quote examples of the way the writer of the first passage has used language to convey particular effects, and to comment on why your examples are powerful. This is a two-part question for which you are expected to answer in about one side of writing, which includes about 5 examples for each part.

13 Scan the passage, highlighting the information given about Luxor.

> ▼ *Exam tip!*
>
> Highlight only the essential points in a text – the key words – rather than whole sentences or paragraphs. When selecting material for a summary task, avoid including
> - repetitions
> - minor details
> - quotations or **direct speech**
> - **descriptive imagery**
> - examples
> - lists

14 Make a grid as shown below and put your highlighted notes into it. Then **paraphrase** them (put them into your own words) as far as possible. Try to make your own phrases shorter than the ones from the text, since summary is a process of reduction.

Highlighted phrase	Own words
barren, rubble-strewn desert	rubbish-covered wasteland

▼ *Exam tip!*

If you are not sure what a particular word means, it is safer not to change it, although you can still change other words in the phrase. Some technical words do not have synonyms and therefore cannot be changed, e.g. *irrigation*.

15 Use your answers to Exercises 5 and 13 to summarise the characteristics of (a) Luxor and (b) Corsica in about half a side of writing. Use one paragraph for each place.

▼ *Exam tip!*

You don't have time in the exam to write a first draft of a summary, so group and order your material before you begin to write. The best way to do this is by bracketing and numbering your list of notes. Do not confuse a summary with a commentary: you are not required to present information in the same order as in the passage, to compare the passages or to give your views on the material.

16 With your partner, discuss what you already know or think about the following topics:

a Robinson Crusoe
b desert islands
c books, films or television series set on desert islands
d survival techniques

17 Read the text below, which is an extract from a novel written in 1719 as a series of diary entries.

Robinson Crusoe

September 30, 1659. I, poor miserable Robinson Crusoe, being shipwrecked, during a dreadful storm, came on shore on this dismal unfortunate island, which I called the Island of Despair, all the rest of the ship's company being drowned, and myself almost dead.

All the rest of that day I spent in afflicting myself at the dismal circumstances I was brought to, viz. I had neither food, house, clothes, weapon, or place to fly to; and in despair of any relief, saw nothing but death before me; either that I should be devoured by wild beasts, murdered by savages, or starved to death for want of food. At the approach of night, I slept in a tree for fear of wild creatures, but slept soundly, though it rained all night.

From the 1st of October to the 24th. All these days entirely spent in many several voyages to get all I could out of the ship, which I brought on shore, every tide of flood, upon rafts. Much rain also in these days, though with some intervals of fair weather; but, it seems, this was the rainy season.

October 26. I walked about the shore almost all day to find out a place to fix my habitation, greatly concerned to secure myself from an attack in the night, either from wild beasts or men. Towards night I fixed upon a proper place under a rock, and marked out a semicircle for my encampment, which I resolved to strengthen with a work, wall, or fortification…

The 31st, in the morning, I went out into the island with my gun to see for some food, and discover the country; when I killed a she-goat, and her kid followed me home, which I afterwards killed also, because it would not feed.

November 1. I set up my tent under a rock, and lay there for the first night, making it as large as I could, with stakes driven in to swing my hammock upon.

November 17. This day I began to dig behind my tent into the rock. Note, three things I wanted exceedingly for this work, viz. a pick-axe, a shovel, and a wheel-barrow or basket; so I ceased my work, and began to consider how to supply that want and make me some tools. A spade was so absolutely necessary, that indeed I could nothing effectually without it; but what kind of one to make, I knew not.

January 1. Very hot still, but I went abroad early and late with my gun, and lay still in the middle of the day. This evening, going farther into the valleys which lay towards the centre of the island, I found there was plenty of goats, though exceeding shy, and hard to come at. However, I resolved to try if I could not bring my dog to hunt them down.

January 2. Accordingly, the next day, I went out with my dog, and set him upon the goats; but I was mistaken, for they all faced about upon the dog; and he knew his danger too well, for he would not come near them.

January 3. I began my fence or wall; which being still fearful of my being attacked by somebody, I resolved to make very thick and strong.

All this time I worked very hard, the rains hindering me many days, nay, sometimes weeks together; but I thought I should never be perfectly secure till this wall was finished. And it is scarce credible what inexpressible labour everything was done with, especially the bringing piles out of the woods, and driving them into the ground; for I made them much bigger than I need to have done.

In the next place, I was at a great loss for candle; so that as soon as ever it was dark, which was generally by seven o'clock, I was obliged to go to bed.

Source: Adapted from Daniel Defoe, *Robinson Crusoe*

18 In one sentence, describe what you have learned about the situation of Robinson Crusoe on the Island of Despair by answering these questions in any order:

- Who?
- What?
- When?
- Where?
- Why?
- How?

19 After highlighting the relevant material in the text, write a one-paragraph summary, in modern English, of Robinson Crusoe's

- needs
- difficulties
- fears
- concerns
- disappointments

> ▼ *Exam tip!*
>
> Rather than using one sentence for each point, try to combine material into complex sentences. Avoid beginning each sentence the same way or repeating the same structure, e.g. don't start every sentence with *He*, and avoid the overuse of *and*. Before you write each sentence, plan in your head its **structure** and style. Check your summary for accuracy of expression, omissions and repetitions.

20 With your partner, list future incidents or problems which Robinson Crusoe may face later in the novel, based on evidence in the extract. Share and support your predictions with the rest of the class.

21 In small groups, consider which things Robinson Crusoe would have liked to have with him. List three items and give the reasons, according to the extract, why they would be useful.

Further practice

a You have become stranded on a desert island! Write a description of the imaginary island. Think about its landscape, climate, vegetation, wildlife, food and water sources. You can use information from the island passages in Exercises 3 and 17 of this unit.

b List the main features of your home town or rural area. Use the list to write an information leaflet for tourists, in which your notes appear as bullet points. Group the points, divide them into sections, and give a topic heading to each section (e.g. *Things to see*). The passage in Exercise 6 will help you.

c From what you have read in this unit, would you rather visit Corsica, Cape Town or Luxor? Give reasons for your preference, using evidence from the texts.

> ▼ *Exam tip!*
>
> Paper 2 question 2 asks candidates to select the language from a passage which gives a particular impression to the reader. In addition to quoting a range of short examples (often one word for each), you should also make clear that you understand both their meaning and their effect. In the exercise above, your reasons for preferring a destination should be linked to the descriptive phrases which make it seem attractive.

Unit 2: *Directed writing*

This unit prepares for directed writing by considering audience and style; it focuses on diary- and letter-writing tasks.

❶ Discuss the following questions with your partner:

    a How would you define 'extreme sports'?
    b What examples can you think of?
    c What kind of people are attracted to them?
    d What makes them attractive?

❷ Read the following article. It is a newspaper review of a **non-fiction** book about an Arctic tragedy.

The big chill

Arctic explorers are a breed apart, inevitably drawn, it would seem, by tragedy and the poetry of a 'good end'. Consider Shackleton. Having narrowly survived the loss of his ship, the *Endurance*, when it was crushed by ice in the Weddell Sea, he later died aboard the *Quest*, another Antarctic no-hoper, in 1922. Scott, of course, perished ten years earlier just a few miles from his base camp, having failed by a whisker to reach the South Pole. Amundsen, who beat his rival by just a couple of days, went on to die in an Arctic air crash.

Good chaps, each and every one of them. But what was it all about? In *The Ice Master*, an appropriately chilling account of the voyage of the *Karluk*, lead-ship of a doomed Arctic expedition in 1913–14, the motivation of those taking part seems to have been fool-hardy at best. Vilhjalmur Stefansson, a Canadian of Nordic extraction, was an anthropologist and ethnologist who, for reasons best known to himself, believed that under the Arctic ice there lay a Lost Continent, a kind of wintry Atlantis, the discovery of which would make him famous. In reality, of course, there is no missing land-mass; the Arctic Ocean is just what its name implies. But to the impatient Stefansson, the fact that there was, literally, no solid ground for his belief was defeatist talk.

Hiring a steely skipper, Captain Bob Bartlett, Stefansson ordered the *Karluk* to sea from Victoria in British Columbia on June 17, 1913. Few of his men had real Arctic experience. The 'scientists' on board knew very little of the trials ahead. The ship itself was a retired whaler, made of wood, staggeringly unsuited to its new purpose.

The crew, it transpires, had an eerie premonition of their fate. Stuck fast in the Alaskan floes, they were 'transfixed' by the diaries of George Washington De Long, another of their breed, who had died, along with all his men, in 1881. De Long's ship, the *Jeanette*, had been crushed by ice in almost exactly the same reach of the Arctic Ocean as the *Karluk*. One hundred and forty days passed before cold and starvation claimed the last of the expedition's victims.

Jennifer Niven, formerly a screenwriter, assembles her characters with all the skill of an experienced novelist. Both of the principals are carefully drawn. There is Bartlett, an energetic, skilful mariner, big in every way, with a booming voice and a love for literature and women. Stefansson, by contrast, comes across as an egotist of monstrous proportions. Charming, silver-tongued and handsome, he cared little for those under his command.

Locked together on the diminutive ship, the crew of the *Karluk* watched and listened in horror as the frozen sea closed in around them. The staff and officers gathered nightly in the saloon for Victrola concerts, choosing from among more than 200 records. As the gloom grew ever deeper, the lure of the library, with its terrible account of the fate of the *Jeanette*, increased by day.

Stefansson cracked first. Loading up a dog-sledge, he and several others headed off into the night, ostensibly to hunt for food. Others would go to pieces later. Matters came to a head on January 10 when, with a thunderous roar, the ice broke through the ship's hull, forcing the captain to give the order to abandon ship.

In all, 16 men were to die, but Bartlett emerged as the true hero of the hour. Niven's account – always alive to the nuances of human strength as well as weakness – is at its strongest as she recounts his ghastly journey through the Arctic winter in search of help, and his equally determined quest for his lost crewmen when he at last found sanctuary in Siberia. Those who survived long enough for him to find them numbered a lucky 13, including two Eskimo girls and McKinlay, who ever after regarded his captain as 'honest, fearless, reliable, loyal, everything a man should be'.

Stefansson, needless to say, survived as well. Having spectacularly betrayed his comrades, he went on to map and discover several Arctic islands. Collecting a medal for his achievements, he made no mention of the *Karluk*, its crew or the men who were lost.

Source: Adapted from *The Sunday Times*, 19 November 2000

3 With your partner, answer the following questions:

    a Why are book reviews published in newspapers?
    b Who do you think writes them and why?
    c Who do you think reads them and why?
    d Who benefits from the review and how?
    e Who would be interested in reading *The Ice Master*?

4 Publishers promote their new books by printing **blurbs** (brief descriptions) on their back covers. Write a blurb for *The Ice Master*, using three short paragraphs. You need to appeal to your audience and persuade them to buy the book.

- Refer to the background of the expedition and its participants.
- Describe the crisis situation the book deals with.
- Refer to specific incidents which make the book sound exciting.

> ▼ *Exam tip!*
>
> Directed writing questions ask you to respond to 'one or more short texts' by writing a piece of about $1\frac{1}{2}$ to 2 sides in a particular style, using the information in the text(s). You will be assessed on your ability to 'use and develop the given information in another form' using 'a range of appropriate vocabulary' (W3).

5 Highlight all dates and time references in the article. Then list the events in **chronological** order (the order in which they occurred), together with their date or duration, in a grid as shown below. This will give you a sense of the overall time scheme, which will help you later. An example has been given.

Event	Time
Jeanette crushed	1881

6 Read the extracts from the diary on page 11 of the Antarctic explorer Robert Falcon Scott (who is mentioned in the article in Exercise 2). On 16 January 1912, he found that the Norwegian explorer Roald Amundsen had beaten him to the South Pole.

7 With your partner, list the common characteristics of the style of writing used in diaries (also remember the diary extract in Exercise 17 of Unit 1). Diaries are obviously written in the first person – using *I* or *we* – but what can you say about the following?

- tense
- register
- vocabulary level
- sentence length
- sentence type
- content

Scott's diary

17th Jan: Great God! This is an awful place and terrible enough for us to have laboured to it without the reward of priority. Well, it is something to have got here, and the wind may be our friend tomorrow.

18th Jan: Well, we have turned our back now on the goal of our ambition with sore feelings and must face 800 miles of solid dragging – and goodbye to the daydreams!

23rd Jan: I don't like the look of it. Is the weather breaking up? If so God help us, with the tremendous summit journey and scant food.

18th Feb: Pray God we get better travelling as we are not so fit as we were and the season advances apace.

5th Mar: God help us, we can't keep up this pulling, that is certain. Among ourselves we are unendingly cheerful, but what each man feels in his heart I can only guess.

29th Mar: It seems a pity, but I do not think I can write more. R. Scott. For God's sake look after our people.

8 Imagine you are Captain Bob Bartlett in the article in Exercise 2. Write three diary entries, with dates, for the winter period of 1913–14, from the freezing of the sea to when you abandon ship.

Use the time grid from Exercise 5 to help you. Do not simply retell the story. Write about one side, in an appropriate style, and refer to the following:

- previous events and the original goal of the expedition
- Stefansson's character and behaviour
- the mood of the crew and their fears
- how the crew passed the time
- what happened to the *Karluk*
- the journey you are about to face
- your thoughts and feelings about the future

> ▼ *Exam tip!*
>
> 'Directed writing' means writing for the purpose and audience appropriate to the task which has been set. Consider the **register** (form of language) and style (general expression) required, and adapt your wording rather than simply giving a list of points from the text. You will be rewarded for original language as well as for your ability to switch **genres**.

9 The next passage concerns mountaineering. Discuss these questions with your partner:

a How do you feel about mountains?
b What makes some people determined to get to the top of them?
c What can go wrong during a climbing expedition?
d What do you think the title 'A rock and a hard place' means?

10 Read the article below, from a Sunday newspaper magazine, which concerns the death of a mountain climber.

A ROCK AND A HARD PLACE

Alison Hargreaves faced the toughest decision of her career. It was August 6: she had spent six weeks on K2 and had already failed in two summit bids. Now, should she stay and give it one more try? Or call it a day and go home?

The situation was as bleak as could be. Alison was back at base camp, its cluster of red and yellow tents pitched unevenly among the ice and boulders of the Godwin-Austen Glacier. Towering 12,000 ft above was K2 itself, shrouded in grey, wind-tossed clouds. It was bitterly cold and raining and, says the American climber Richard Celsi, Alison was in tears.

By Celsi's account, Alison had changed her mind a dozen times. Now she was utterly torn. She wanted to fulfil her dream of climbing K2, adding it to Everest to become the only British woman to have reached the world's two highest summits. And she desperately wanted to be back with her children, Tom, six, and Kate, four.

The previous night she seemed to have made up her mind to leave. She had packed her equipment and said goodbye to the climbers who were staying. Her porters were due to leave at 7 a.m. and Alison had a flight booked from Islamabad in a week's time. 'It was done,' says Celsi. 'She was going home.'

But early that morning, Alison reopened the question once again, drinking endless cups of coffee with Celsi as she turned it over and over in her mind. 'It was a very emotional thing for her,' says Celsi. 'She really went through a lot of things.' Finally, just 15 minutes before the porters were due to depart, she told Celsi she had decided to stay, reasoning that, since she had been away for so long, one more week wouldn't matter. 'She said it was logical to give the weather a chance to clear.'

Alison hugged Celsi and thanked him profusely for his help. In some haste, her equipment was retrieved. Celsi himself was leaving, and Alison gave him some letters and a fax saying she had decided to give K2 'one more try'.

As he set off down the glacier, Celsi turned to look back at Alison, and saw her waving to him through the drifting rain. 'She seemed in good spirits,' he recalls. 'She had made her decision.'

Four days later Alison and a group of climbers left base camp for their summit bid. By August 12, they had reached Camp Four on a sloping snow-field known as the Shoulder, 2,000 ft below the summit. They set off before dawn the next morning, climbing a steep gully called the Bottleneck, passing beneath an unstable wall of ice pinnacles and finally emerging on the summit ridge.

At 6.30 p.m. the climbers in base camp received a radio call from the summit. Alison and three others had reached the top, and another two were about to arrive. The caller, a Spanish climber, added that there was no wind but it was bitterly cold, and they were about to start their descent. There was no further word.

An hour later the upper reaches of K2 were hit by hurricane-force winds. As they edged their way back down the summit ridge, Alison and her companions stood no chance. She was plucked from the ridge by the wind and hurled down K2's monumental South Face.

The next morning two Spanish climbers, Pepe Garces and Lorenzo Ortas, who had survived the storm at Camp Four, were descending the mountain suffering from frostbite and exhaustion. Some 3,000 ft below the summit they found a blood-stained anorak lying in the snow. They also saw three slide-marks leading towards the edge of an ice cliff. But above the cliff, some 600 ft away, they saw a body resting in a hollow. 'I recognised the red clothing,' Ortas says. 'I knew it was Alison.'

*   *   *   *   *

At 33, after a mercurial climbing career, Alison had become an icon – a symbol of what women could achieve. For some her death represented a betrayal of motherhood, for others a paradigm of the dilemmas faced by mothers seeking a career.

Alison had been bemused by the publicity her Everest climb attracted, saying: 'The whole thing is much bigger than I can handle.' But she was worthy of her acclaim. Her Everest ascent in May – alone and without using supplementary oxygen or porters – was a supreme moment of the sport. Just 5 ft 4 in and with an easy smile, she impressed people with her friendliness, modesty and charm. Some, accustomed to the ruthless egos of some leading male mountaineers, were relieved to find her so *normal*.

Yet Alison was far more complex than her image revealed. The climber who exulted in her triumph on Everest could be racked with doubt. She could be talkative and outgoing – or reticent and closed. She was eager to show that she was self-sufficient, yet ardent for approval and acclaim. And while her motherhood attained symbolic status, her marriage was deeply troubled.

The most profound contradiction lay in her replies when asked the perennial question of why she climbed. She said she did so because she had something to prove – then added that, after each summit, she felt she had to prove herself again. So what was Alison trying to prove, and why was she never satisfied? And is it true that her ceaseless quest led inevitably to a reckless death?

Source: *The Sunday Times,* 3 December 1995

⓫ With your partner, work on the following tasks:

    a Think of and list adjectives which you could use to describe the character of Alison Hargreaves.

    b Agree on and list the characteristics of the writing style commonly used for informal letters.

⓬ Write Alison Hargreaves' last letter to her parents after deciding to stay. Use an appropriate style, and about 250 words. Begin *Dear Mum and Dad… .* Refer to the following:

- her difficult decision and how she made it
- conditions on K2
- her ambitions and expectations
- her fellow climbers
- her feelings about her family

⓭ What do the experiences of the crew of the *Karluk* have in common with those of the K2 climbers? List the points you would use in responding to this question, after you have underlined the key words in the question.

▼ *Exam tip!*

You must understand exactly what a task requires, and cover all the material needed for a question with more than one part. It's a good habit to underline the important words in an exam question and to check that you have followed the instructions exactly. For instance, a word like *what*, which is different from *why* or *how*, gives focus to Summary, Directed writing and Composition responses.

14 Read the leaflet, which gives information about a youth outdoor-pursuits programme. It is called 'The Duke of Edinburgh's Award' or 'The International Award'.

What is it?

The Duke of Edinburgh's Award is a voluntary, non-competitive programme of practical, cultural and adventurous activities, designed to support the personal and social development of young people aged 14–25, regardless of gender, background or ability. It offers an individual challenge and encourages young people to undertake exciting, constructive, challenging and enjoyable activities in their free time.

What does the Programme consist of?

It is a four Section programme with three progressive levels:
- Bronze (for those aged 14 and over)
- Silver (for those aged 15 and over) and
- Gold (for those aged 16 and over)

The Sections involve:
- **Service** Helping other people in the local community
- **Expeditions** Training for, planning and completing a journey on foot or horseback, by boat or cycle
- **Skills** Covering almost any hobby, skill or interest
- **Physical Recreation** Sport, dance and fitness
- **Residential Project** (Gold Award only) A purposeful enterprise with people not previously known to the Participant

What are the benefits of involvement?

The Award is widely recognised by educationalists and employers. Some of the benefits to young people include developing or discovering:
- A sense of achievement
- New skills and interests
- Self-confidence and self-reliance
- Leadership skills and abilities
- Exciting opportunities
- Friendship
- Experience of teamwork and decision making
- A network of local, national and international connections
- Enjoyment

15 Select the relevant material in the text, then use it to write the script for a talk of about one side, addressed to a group of fellow students. Explain the Award Programme and encourage them to take part.

- Summarise the rules and structure of the programme.
- Explain the aims and what is involved.
- Comment on the benefits and give examples.

⑯ Give your talk to the class, and be prepared to answer any questions your audience asks about the Programme.

⑰ With your partner, look back at the list of extreme sports which you made in Exercise 1b. Can you now add some more? Discuss which ones you would or would not be prepared to try, giving reasons.

⑱ Read the advertisement for a training course in hang-gliding.

Discover Hang-gliding at Lookout Mountain

Try Hang-gliding Once for memories that last a lifetime! Soar like an eagle in this purest form of flight! In-flight photos available. Fly with a professional certified instructor pilot by your side for a bird's eye view of beautiful Lookout Mountain. This flight is to 2,000 feet. 12 to 20 minutes of flying time. Satisfaction guaranteed and we mean it!

Pilots enjoy consistently good flying and training at Lookout. An easy cliff launch and 20 miles of ridge provide great soaring for low-time pilots. No other flight park can match our people, facilities, diversity, dedication and history of excellence. Our complete desire is to help you realize your flying dreams and hang-gliding goals.

Lookout Mountain Flight Park is the largest and most successful full-time hang-gliding school and resort in the United States. We teach and certify more hang-glider pilots than any other school in the country. We offer the most comprehensive training facility on a 44-acre mountain retreat with camping and lodging conveniently located in our landing zone. Other amenities include swimming pool, volleyball court, clubhouse, bathhouse, bunkhouse, cabins and shaded pavilions. We've been teaching people to fly on our gently sloping training hills since 1978. Lookout Mountain Flight Park is America's #1 choice.

Discovery Tandem Flight $139   **Weekend Package $399**

Source: http://www.hangglide.com

⑲ What are the stylistic features of written advertisements? Give examples of each from the passage above, and explain how they aim to persuade.

▼ *Exam tip!*

Advertisements aim to persuade using imperative verbs, exclamations, **clichés**, short/non-sentences, contractions, lists, comparatives and superlatives, the personal pronouns *we* and *our*, multiple adjectives, and statistics. These features make the text as easy as possible to read and understand, and entice and pressurise the reader into accepting the offered product.

20 Write an informal letter of one side to a friend, suggesting that you both go on the training course. (Pretend it is in your own country.)

- Give all the factual information.
- Describe your impression of the school.
- Give reasons why you think it would be a good idea.

> ▼ *Exam tip!*
>
> Informal letters or e-mails tend to use contractions (e.g. *can't*, *uni*, *ok*), **abbreviations**, phonetic spelling and **colloquial** expressions (e.g. *no way*, *go clubbing*) as if the writer is speaking aloud to the recipient, with whom s/he has a casual relationship. You must judge from the task how informal it is appropriate for your response to be, but it is likely that a degree of formality is required in the Directed writing component, as in all the other exam tasks. If you are asked to write a letter to a friend or relative in Paper 1 question 2 or Paper 3 question 1, you may respond in a fairly informal style, but not one which uses slang, jargon or non-sentences, or which does not use paragraphs.

21 Formal letters which aim to *persuade* or *argue* have the following format, which you would use when writing for official or business purposes to someone whom you have never met.

Dear Madam/Sir (or the official position)
or
Dear Mr/Ms Surname (if you know his/her name)

Section 1: Reason for writing / topic of letter
Section 2: Background to and details of request, complaint, issue
Section 3: Conclusion, threat, thanks, prediction, advice, warning

Yours faithfully (if you have not addressed the recipient by name)
or
Yours sincerely (if you have addressed the recipient by name)

Example of letter text

I am writing to you because of an incident I witnessed recently in one of your stores, which made me feel angry and embarrassed.

Last Saturday afternoon I was with my family in your Buenos Aires branch, shopping for toys. An elderly man, who was alone, collapsed on the floor, and a nearby customer asked for an ambulance to be called. The member of staff at the pay counter said he was too busy, suggesting that the customer should use her mobile phone instead. Although the store was very busy that day, I do not believe this was an acceptable response from the member of staff, and my children and some foreign tourists were shocked by the lack of concern which it revealed.

Unless such behaviour is your company policy, it seems that there is a need for your employees to be better trained in customer service, as this kind of incident damages your reputation with the public.

Exam tip! See next page ▶

Formal letters differ from informal letters in register and in having a clear and conventional structure: usually one paragraph per section, although the middle section can extend over two or three paragraphs. The tone of a formal letter is impersonal and polite – even when complaining – and the language is formal, i.e. in complex sentences and without contractions, abbreviations or colloquialisms. You may be asked to write a formal letter in response to question 1 in Paper 2 or Paper 3. Whereas in Paper 1 you are expected to 'select, analyse and evaluate what is relevant to specific purposes' (R3), in the Directed Writing task in Paper 3 you are required to make full use of the stimulus material provided to show that you are able to write in a 'language and register appropriate to audience and context' (W4). It is not necessary to date or give addresses in an exam letter.

22 Write a letter of about one side to the editor of a local newspaper, giving your views on extreme sports after a recent tragic incident in your area. You may argue either that extreme sports should be allowed or that they should be banned.

Use the ideas which you collected in Exercise 1. Refer to the recent incident in your opening paragraph.

23 In small groups, exchange and read each other's letters as preparation for a class discussion on the topic of *Extreme sports*.

Further practice

a   Describe, as if in an informal letter, a sport of which you are fond, either as a spectator or as a participant, to someone who knows nothing about it. Include a brief explanation of the rules.

b   Imagine that you and your friend went on the hang-gliding training course at Lookout Mountain and were not satisfied. Write a letter of complaint to the company and ask for your money back. Include references to the advertisement in Exercise 18.

c   Imagine that you are on a Duke of Edinburgh's Award expedition which has met with unforeseen difficulties. Write a one-side diary entry describing your location, situation, thoughts and feelings.

Unit 3: Composition

This unit introduces the continuous writing component of the exam and focuses on descriptive skills, particularly the use of adjectives and imagery.

❶ Four types of composition are assessed in the exam and coursework. Can you match the type of writing to its definition in the list below? Does your partner agree?

descriptive   narrative   discursive   argumentative

- discusses something informatively from different viewpoints
- tries to convince the reader that an opinion is correct
- relates a pattern of events
- tries to enable the reader to visualise something

❷ The following titles are typical Composition titles. Next to each, write which of the four types you think it is. Discuss with your partner; there may be more than one answer in some cases.

a *The time of my life*
b *Travel broadens the mind*
c *Great inventions*
d *Write a story which involves a big meal.*
e *What do you think life will be like fifty years from now?*
f *My first memory*
g *Peace*
h *The tree*

> **▼** *Exam tip!*
>
> In Paper 3 you will choose one from six composition titles covering the different types. Get to know which kind of writing you are best at, since it is unusual for someone to be equally good at all of them. An important exam technique is knowing how to choose the right composition question.
>
> Instead of writing an exam composition, you can submit school-based coursework. This consists of three pieces of 500–800 words each. Although the coursework process and the tasks differ from the exam questions, the skills needed to produce appropriate, high-quality continuous writing responses are the same.

❸ Are the following statements about descriptive writing true or false?

a Descriptive writing must be based on the truth.
b You need a wide vocabulary to be good at descriptions.
c It is difficult to make descriptive writing interesting.

d Descriptive writing is the easiest choice for candidates in the exam.

e You should only use the sense of sight when you describe something.

Discuss your views with the rest of the class and your teacher.

> ▼ *Exam tip!*
>
> Descriptive compositions may be real or imagined, but try to base your description on an actual memory or experience as your response will then be more authentic and original, and it will be easier for you to think of material. It is difficult to engage readers in descriptive writing, and in order to do so you should: choose unusual vocabulary; use as many of the five senses as possible; employ multiple adjectives, **similes** and **metaphors**; vary your sentence length; avoid repetition of any kind; create sound effects.

4 Read this paragraph from *Hard Times,* by Charles Dickens, which describes an industrial town in northern England in the nineteenth century.

It was a town of red brick, or of brick that would have been red if the smoke and ashes had allowed it; but, as matters stood, it was a town of unnatural red and black like the painted face of a savage. It was a town of machinery and tall chimneys, out of which interminable serpents of smoke trailed themselves for ever and ever, and never got uncoiled. It had a black canal in it, and a river that ran purple with ill-smelling dye, and vast piles of building full of windows where there was a rattling and a trembling all day long, and where the piston of the steam-engine worked monotonously up and down, like the head of an elephant in a state of melancholy madness. It contained several large streets all very like one another, and many small streets still more like one another, inhabited by people equally like one another, who all went in and out at the same hours, with the same sound upon the same pavements, to do the same work, and to whom every day was the same as yesterday and tomorrow, and every year the counterpart of the last and next.

5 Underline the words/**phrases** which create atmosphere. Agree with your partner which adjectives are the main contributors to the feeling of this extract.

6 Write words, including colours, which come to mind when you consider the following moods or atmospheres:

- loneliness
- decay
- celebration
- tranquillity
- fear

7 Atmosphere can best be created by appealing to all five senses: sight, sound, smell, touch, taste. Colour, size and shape are important elements in descriptive writing too.

Write a paragraph covering as many senses as possible, to describe each of the following:

a a street market in summer
b an outdoor festival in winter

Read some of your paragraphs to the class for comparison and comments.

8 To widen your descriptive vocabulary, look up the following adjectives in a dictionary and record the words and definitions in your personal vocabulary list. Then use each word in a sentence of your own to show you understand what it means.

a iridescent   d perpendicular
b flamboyant   e exhilarating
c scintillating   f exotic

9 Replace the underlined words in the following sentences with more unusual and ambitious adjectives.

a The students had a <u>good</u> day out.
b The weather yesterday was <u>bad</u>.
c I think your new dress is very <u>nice</u>.
d The film I saw last night was <u>awful</u>.
e What a <u>pretty</u> view!

10 Adjectives are the key to effective descriptive writing, in which nouns need to be qualified by at least one adjective, preferably more.

Add two adjectives before each noun in each of the following phrases. Think of adjectives with interesting sounds and avoid clichés (obvious and common phrases such as *busy street* or *delicious food*). Size adjectives go first and colour adjectives second in normal adjectival order, e.g. *the huge, green, slimy monster*.

a the house on the corner of the street
b the girl with the dog in the garden
c the car in the car park by the river
d the meal in the restaurant in the city centre
e the students in the school in the suburb

Now extend each of the phrases, with your extra adjectives, into full sentences with verbs and adverbs which are precise and vivid.

11 With your partner, list all the verbs you know which refer to a manner of walking, e.g. *shuffled*. Now use a thesaurus to add to your list. See which pair in the class can get the longest list in 10 minutes. (Make sure that you understand what the words mean and that they are still in common use.) Write the words which are new to you in your personal vocabulary list.

> ▼ *Exam tip!*
>
> *The man was walking along the street* is much less effective than *The ancient bearded tramp in his tattered navy overcoat and filthy unmatched shoes was shuffling along the damp and littered pavement.* Verbs of locomotion describe more than just movement: they can convey the gender, age, social status, health, mood and personality of the character.

12 A haiku is a kind of descriptive poem. Here are two examples:

> *Strangely yellow bird*
> *At a desert waterhole*
> *Dips its beak and drinks*

> *Gold and scarlet leaves*
> *Rustle in the lively breeze*
> *In the high mountains*

Haikus must have five syllables in the first and third lines, and seven syllables in the middle line. They aim to describe a beautiful or impressive natural moment.

Write haikus for the pictures below. Draft and edit in order to arrive at the best possible versions to read out to the class. Remember to use unusual and specific vocabulary, and think about sound effects.

13 Read the passage below from *My Family and Other Animals,* by Gerald Durrell, which describes a house on the Greek island of Corfu.

The villa was small and square, standing in its tiny garden with an air of pink-faced determination. Its shutters had been faded by the sun to a delicate creamy-green, cracked and bubbled in places. The garden, surrounded by tall fuchsia hedges, had the flower-beds worked in complicated geometrical patterns, marked with smooth white stones. The white cobbled paths, scarcely as wide as a rake's head, wound laboriously round beds hardly larger than a big straw hat, beds in the shape of stars, half-moons, triangles, and circles, all overgrown with a shaggy tangle of flowers run wild. Roses dropped petals that seemed as big and smooth as saucers, flame-red, moon-white, glossy, and unwrinkled; marigolds like broods of shaggy suns stood watching their parent's progress through the sky. In the low growth the pansies pushed their velvety, innocent faces through the leaves, and the violets drooped sorrowfully under their heart-shaped leaves. The bougainvillaea that sprawled luxuriously over the tiny front balcony was hung, as though for a carnival, with its lantern-shaped magenta flowers. In the darkness of the fuchsia hedge a thousand ballerina-like blooms quivered expectantly. The warm air was thick with the scent of a hundred dying flowers, and full of the gentle, soothing whisper and murmur of insects. As soon as we saw it, we wanted to live there – it was as though the villa had been standing there waiting for our arrival. We felt we had come home.

14 You will have noticed a large number of adjectives in this passage. With your partner, answer the following questions:

a What can you say about the type of adjectives used?
b Why do you think there are so many hyphenated compound adjectives?
c Underline the adverbs. How are they used?
d Can you find evidence of personification (describing things as if they were people)?
e How else has the passage been made vivid?

15 With your partner, discuss the following pairs of sentences. In each pair, tick the sentence which is more effective, and be prepared to explain your choice.

a It was autumn and the trees were aflame.
It was autumn and the leaves were reddish-brown.
b The old man's face was wrinkled.
The old man's face was like a withered apple.
c Her laugh tinkled like ice in a glass.
Her laugh was high-pitched.
d The waiting passengers pushed onto the train.
The waiting passengers stormed the train.
e The rain drummed on the roof.
The rain beat loudly on the roof.

16 It is likely that in Exercise 15 you preferred the sentences which contain imagery. Here are more examples:

   a The hail stung the windows.
   b The sun stalked across the fields, as stealthily as a tiger.
   c The hillside bloomed with scarlet men marching.
   d Life's but a walking shadow.
   e The sea is like a giant, grey, hungry dog.
   f A lake is a river curled and asleep like a snake.

Write *S* or *M* next to each sentence, according to whether you think it is a simile or a metaphor. Does your partner agree? Which image do you find the most effective as description, and why?

17 Complete the following similes and metaphors using original, but also appropriate, comparisons.

   a The baby's skin was as soft as…
   b He leaped across the stream like…
   c The train … its way through the mountain pass.
   d She is as dangerous as a…
   e The soldiers marched as if they…

18 Rewrite the following sentences to make the descriptions more detailed and specific by using imagery.

   a The child was crying.
   b The house looked empty.
   c It started to rain.
   d The football stadium was crowded.
   e The woman got angry.

19 To test how effective a piece of descriptive writing is, try to draw what is being described. As you read the passage below and on page 24 from Ray Bradbury's *A Sound of Thunder*, draw the Tyrannosaurus rex.

It came on great, oiled, resilient, striding legs. It towered twenty feet above trees, a huge evil god, folding its delicate watchmaker's claws to its oily, reptilian chest. Each lower leg was a piston, a thousand pounds of white bone sunk in thick ropes of muscle, sheathed over in a gleam of pebbled skin like the mail of a terrible warrior. Each thigh was a ton of meat, ivory and steel mesh. And from the great breathing cage of the upper body those two delicate arms dangled out in front, arms with hands which might pick up and examine men like toys, while the snake neck coiled. And the head, a ton of sculptured stone itself, lifted easily upon the sky. Its mouth gaped, exposing a fence of teeth like daggers. Its eyes rolled, ostrich eggs, empty of all expression save hunger.

It ran, its pelvic bones crushing aside trees and bushes, its taloned feet clawing damp earth, leaving prints six inches deep wherever it settled its weight. It ran with a gliding ballet step, far too poised and balanced for its ten tons. It moved into a sunlit arena, warily, its beautiful reptile hands feeling the air.

Is your picture complete? Compare it with your partner's and, if they differ, try to justify your picture by referring to descriptive details in the passage.

20 Describe a picture, photograph or postcard (given to you by your teacher or brought from home) of a countryside or town scene, while your partner – who must not be allowed to see your picture – draws what you are describing. Then draw what your partner describes. Compare drawings with the original pictures to see how accurate your descriptions were. You may be amused!

21 Imagine you are a Martian who has landed on earth. Describe to the rest of the class (your fellow Martians) a place you have visited and what happens there. You cannot mention the actual name of the place! You might choose

- a school
- an athletics stadium
- an airport

- a hospital
- a theatre
- a bowling alley

22 Look again at the first and last sentences of the passage in Exercise 13. Discuss with your partner whether they are effective, giving reasons.

> ▼ *Exam tip!*
>
> Effective openings and endings always make a good impression in a composition. A strong opening may set the scene and refer to time, place, season, weather; a strong ending may draw a conclusion or refer back to the title or the beginning of the description.

23 With your partner, guess whether the following are openings or endings to pieces of descriptive writing.

a It was the summer of 1996 and there had been a heat wave in Brasilia for over a week.
b As far as I'm concerned, the future is not something to look forward to.
c The impression will stay in my mind for the rest of my life.
d The trip to Africa was all my grandmother's idea.
e I hadn't really noticed the garden before the day my ball went over the wall.

24 Rank the following openings to descriptive pieces, according to how engaged you feel as a reader (1 = least engaging; 5 = most engaging). Write a comment for each one to explain why you have placed it high or low.

a   Imagine then a flat landscape, dark for the moment, but even so conveying to a girl running in the still deeper shadow cast by the wall an idea of immensity, of distance.

b   I think the best place I have ever visited is the football stadium in my town.

c   When I think of the year 2050, the first thing which comes into my head is a vision of bright lights.

d   The house my family moved to when I was six years old looked like a monster crouching on a hill waiting to pounce on and devour those foolish enough to pass by.

e   It was a fairy-tale turreted castle, which gave the impression that it had a sleeping princess in the attic and a heap of gold treasure in the dungeon, guarded by a fearsome, fiery dragon.

25   Write first and last sentences for a composition on each of the following titles:

a   *Paradise Island*
b   *Home sweet home*
c   *The place which has most affected my life*
d   *Describe a place you visited which was not at all what you expected.*
e   *Jungle*

26   Look at the reasons suggested below why continuous writing – exam composition or coursework – should be planned. Tick the reasons you agree with, and then discuss them as a class.

a   to give your writing structure
b   to build to a climax or conclusion
c   to avoid repetition of material or vocabulary
d   to achieve the required length
e   to check you have made the right choice of title
f   to give focus to your response
g   to ensure you stay relevant to the title
h   to develop your material logically
i   to provide enough support or detail to be convincing
j   to give full coverage to the title
k   to enable you to concentrate on expression and accuracy when writing
l   to make a good impression on the examiner

▼ *Exam tip!*

All of the reasons given above are valid! If after 5 minutes of thinking and planning you don't have at least 8 points to use in your composition, consider switching to a different title and starting again. Up to 10 minutes should be spent planning a composition. Planning has three steps:
• make a list, in a column, of 'topic headings' – i.e. single words or short phrases, each of which can be developed into a paragraph
• add supporting material in note form to each heading
• order the headings logically, using numbers or arrows

Plan a descriptive composition on each of the two photographs below, entitled *Haunted house* and *Crowded market*.

28 Plan the following composition titles. What difference does the definite article and use of the plural make?

   a *The lake*
   b *A place I never want to go back to*
   c *Where I come from*
   d *City street at night*
   e *Mountains*

> ▼ *Exam tip!*
>
> A particular event or time may help to give a focus and structure for a descriptive composition, but you must avoid responding in narrative mode to a descriptive title and remember that the aim of description is to clearly convey a sense of place (or person) and atmosphere.

Further practice

a   Write the composition for which you made the best plan in Exercise 28. Do not take more than one hour. Remember to check your writing when you have finished.

> ▼ *Exam tip!*
>
> Content, structure, style and accuracy all feature in the assessment criteria for Composition. Leave enough time to check your work carefully in the exam. Checking is as important as planning, since it enables you to notice careless errors, missing words or links, and unclear or clumsy expressions. Also remember that to achieve a top grade for 'Style and Accuracy', you must use 'a variety of well-made sentences, including sophisticated complex sentences'.

b   Draw a plan of the perfect house and label it. Use this plan as the basis for a coursework piece or exam-practice composition with the title *My ideal home*.

c   As a coursework draft or for exam practice, write a composition describing either *My nightmare landscape* or *My idea of heaven*.

> ▼ *Exam tip!*
>
> Unlike an exam composition, a piece of writing for coursework should be drafted as well as planned, and it is an IGCSE requirement that a draft of one of the three coursework pieces be included in the portfolio and submitted to the board. It is essential to bear in mind that the downloading and reproducing of unaltered source material for coursework counts as plagiarism.
>
> The purpose of the draft – which should be in continuous prose – is to enable your teacher to comment on general aspects of its structure, length, content and accuracy, so that by following the advice you can improve it in the next and final version. It is pointless to resubmit your draft as your final piece without changing it. However, your teacher is not permitted to point out or correct individual mistakes, so you need to proofread and edit your work carefully before you give it in for assessment.

Unit 4: *Speaking and listening*

This unit develops the skills needed for the optional Speaking and Listening components of the IGCSE examination.

❶ Look at the picture above and discuss with your partner exactly what is happening and why. Think of words that you would use to convey the situation, atmosphere and emotion of the scene. Share them in a class **brainstorm** on the board.

❷ Choose a sport or physical activity that you know something about and prepare to answer the following questions orally. Work with your partner to ask each other these questions after you have thought about your answers.

a   Which activity have you chosen and why?
b   What are the aims of the activity?
c   What environment, equipment, clothing and facilities are needed for this activity?
d   What is the attraction of the activity?
e   What do you know about the background/history of the activity, e.g. when did it start, which countries is it predominantly associated with?

> ▼ *Exam tip!*
>
> For Paper 5 you will choose a speech topic in advance. The teacher/examiner will discuss the subject with you for 6–7 minutes. You must 'Communicate clearly and fluently' and 'Use language and register appropriate to audience and context.'

3 Rehearse silently an explanation of how to play a sport or board game (e.g. tennis or Monopoly).

Use language that is precise and concise, but not too technical. Avoid sentences that are too long or complicated. Be prepared to answer questions about the rules of the game.

After 5 minutes of preparation, your teacher will pick students to talk to the rest of the class, and the class will ask questions.

Here is an example of how **not** to do it!

The rules of cricket

- You have two sides: one out in the field and one in.
- Each man that's in the side that's in goes out and when he's out he comes in and the next man goes in until he's out.
- When they are all out, the side that's out comes in and the side that's been in goes out and tries to get those coming in out.
- Sometimes you get men still in and not out.
- When both sides have been in and out, including the not outs, that's the end of the game.

---

4 Read the description of a hobby on page 30.

5 With your partner, find evidence that this passage is in colloquial spoken rather than formal written English.

▼ *Exam tip!*

Spoken English, especially in an informal register, is likely to contain: idioms, fashionable expressions, contractions, use of *You* and *I*, short sentences, monosyllabic diction, repetition, use of *And*, *But* and *Or* at the beginning of sentences, afterthoughts signified by dashes, asides, exclamations, non-sentences, simple grammatical structures, and active rather than passive verbs.

---

6 If you were the examiner, what questions would you want to ask the speaker about philately? Write a list. Compare it with your partner's.

7 Discuss with your partner the purposes of a **dialogue** (conversation between two or more people). Do you disagree with any of these listed below? Can you add to the list?

- to communicate ideas
- to convey enthusiasm
- to inform the listener
- to share experience
- to establish a relationship with the other person
- to provide amusement or entertainment

Exam tip! See next page ▶

▼ *Exam tip!*   *relates to Exercise 7*

The effect of speaking depends on actions and appearance as well as words. Body language shows attitude and confidence level, and sends messages to the other person, either positive or negative, e.g. folding your arms may make you seem defensive.

Philately

When other people are wasting their money going out with their mates, I'm doing something much more productive. It couldn't be better, really: it educates me, I have something beautiful to show for it, and I make money because the value of what I have is always increasing. What is this marvel? I collect stamps. Postage stamps. The kind that you stick on letters without thinking about it; the kind you casually throw into the bin every day. Perhaps tomorrow you'll think before you do: that little coloured scrap in the corner of the envelope could already be worth thousands. In ten years it could be worth ten times as much. And someone sent it to you for free! I know collectors who have never bought a stamp in their lives, and their collection is worth tens of thousands.

OK, you say, so it doesn't cost anything to tear the corner off an envelope. But how is that educational? Well, just look at the stamps closely. They tell you the history, the geography, the politics, the culture of a country – of all the countries of the world. The first thing you learn is how other people see themselves. The Hungarians call themselves Magyars; Albania is really Shqiperrija. You find scenes from their history, often with dates, names, great events. You find pictures of their country, their houses, their people, their wildlife. You can see history unfolding: here's one from Zanzibar in 1962 when they declared independence; there was a revolution immediately and the new government overprinted it 'Jamhuru'. Overprints are always a treat, because it means a sudden change of events, a surprise. Here are the stamps Britain printed for the 1966 World Cup; and then, miraculously, England won – remember that last goal! – and the stamps were reissued overprinted 'England Winners'. Amazing. Or they can be sad: here's one from Germany in 1923 when the value of the currency was collapsing so fast they were constantly overprinting new values. This one says 'two milliard Marks' – two thousand million Marks – about enough for a small loaf of bread.

I could go on. I've learnt so much about the whole world and all its history. And when the time comes, I will sell my collection and retire on the proceeds. But until then, I shall marvel at these miniature treasures of the designer's and the printer's art. A thing of beauty is a joy for ever.

8 Choose the best advice from each of the pairs below, or justify why you do not agree with either. Use your answers to contribute to a class discussion.

a smile at the examiner / keep a serious expression throughout
b sit up straight / relax in your chair
c wear very casual clothing / dress very formally
d fiddle with something / keep your hands still
e flick your hair back continually / make sure your hair does not cover your face
f wave your arms around when speaking / keep your arms firmly in your lap
g avoid eye contact with the examiner / look the examiner in the eye
h project your voice / talk downwards
i chew gum / do not chew gum

9 Comment on the effect on the listener of someone starting a talk in each of the ways listed below:

a Erm… I think I'll talk about something to do with fish.
b I am a leading expert in computer graphics, so listen and I'll tell you all about it.
c Sub-atomic particles can be subsumed into hadrons and leptons but spin and sense are fundamental criteria for any hierarchical categorisation matrix construct.
d Before I start, I need to explain my life history and how I came to be involved in recycling.
e I'm sure you feel the same way as I do about spiders. I mean, they're just really spooky, right?

▼ *Exam tip!*

The openings in Exercise 9 are all examples of how not to start a speech! To interest and impress the examiner

- be precise in your choice of words
- express yourself concisely
- avoid using jargon
- avoid being casual or familiar
- convey enthusiasm for your topic
- do not sound obsessive

---

10 Read the following recommendations. Mark with a tick those you agree with, and with a cross those you disagree with. Be prepared to defend your decisions.

When discussing their topic candidates should

- say as little as possible
- say as much as possible
- answer questions with monosyllables
- use simple vocabulary
- use short and simple grammatical structures
- use long words and advanced vocabulary
- use complicated grammatical structures

Exam tip! See next page ▶

▼ *Exam tip!*   *relates to Exercise 10*

In both the exam and coursework, avoid the temptation to 'over-talk' or 'under-talk' –
i.e. don't dominate, but say enough for a discussion to take place and for assessment to be
possible. You will be rewarded for your ability to 'employ a range of language devices' and to
'Listen to and respond appropriately to the contributions of others' (S5).

11 Read the following article from a hobbies magazine.

Photography

Photography is enthralling because it is both an art and a science. It is an art over which the photographer has creative control but only to a certain extent: unlike a painter, you can only take photographs of what is there. If the sun is not shining, you cannot photograph sunlight. So you need to find a subject. But the greatest photographs are of subjects that most people would have walked past without noticing. The truly great photographers are those who can see, in their mind's eye, the photograph that they can create through their vision, artistry and skill.

Vision comes first. If you cannot see the potential, you can never be a true photographer. Artistry, by contrast, can be learned and developed; you can read a book or you take lessons. You can learn from a great practitioner. Perhaps the simplest aspect to describe is framing. The human eye has a huge field of view, stretching from horizon to horizon. The lens of a camera, by contrast, has a very restricted field of view. This is both a curse and a blessing. Try as

you might, you cannot capture the sheer scale of the human perspective of the world. But you can, and must, select the image that you are attempting to capture – or rather, to create. Look through the viewfinder: learn to see the world through the lens. Understand the difference it makes when you remove the irrelevant and select only what really matters. That is artistry.

Then comes skill. This is the technical part. Skill is exercised long before you even start to look for a subject: first you must select the kind and model of camera you will use. Will it have advanced features, interchangeable lenses, a motor-wind, a built-in flash, automatic focusing? How much do you want to do manually every time you wish to take a photograph, and how much will you leave to the electronics inside? Then you must choose a make and speed of film. The actual taking of the picture requires choices about exposure and shutter speed. After taking the shot, there are more decisions about developing and printing; every decision makes an enormous difference. Experience teaches you about all of these; there is no other way to learn than to try, possibly to fail, but to learn from the experience and improve. This is what marks out the photographer from those who merely take snapshots. There is always a better photograph that could have been taken – the ultimate photograph, if you like. All photographers pursue this goal of perfection. In the process, though, they take some beautiful photographs that bring them joy thereafter.

12 How does the language of this article differ in register from that of the speech about philately in Exercise 4? With your partner, find examples from the two passages to support your answer.

13 Highlight material in the photography article that you consider suitable for use in a discussion on the same topic. Compare your selected material with your partner's, and discuss the reasons for your choices.

14 Where would you look for information when preparing for a talk? On the following list, tick the resources that you would use in your research, and give reasons for your choices.

- Internet
- newspapers
- television news
- television documentaries
- magazines

- specialist journals
- books or encyclopaedias
- your teacher
- anecdotes of friends or relatives
- own memories or experience

▼ *Exam tip!*

Why not use all the resources listed in Exercise 14? The more sources of information you consult, the more likely it is that your presentation will be
- interesting
- informative
- varied
- original
- memorable

---

15 What will the structure of your presentation be? Put the following questions into a logical order using numbers:

- How long have I been interested/involved in the activity/hobby?
- What is the exact nature/definition of my topic?
- What equipment/environment is necessary?
- What memorable/successful/disastrous moments have occurred?
- What kind of people share my interest in this topic?
- How do I see my future with regard to this particular interest?
- What sparked my interest in this topic?
- What is the physical/emotional appeal of this activity?

▼ *Exam tip!*

Although you are preparing to give a speech, you must not follow a script or try to recite from memory. However, you will feel more confident if you prepare a list of headings on a cue card relating to the different aspects of the topic, as this will enable you to show that you can 'Understand, order and present facts, ideas and opinions', but at the same time appear to be talking naturally. If you choose to give a PowerPoint presentation for Paper 5 (exam) or Paper 6 (coursework), use your laptop and projector to produce visual aids for your audience rather than to provide yourself with a script to be read.

---

16 Using the structure created in Exercise 15, plan headings for one of the following topics for a talk. You do not need to be an expert on a subject to talk about it, but you do need to know something about it.

- *Team sports*
- *Collecting*
- *Making music*
- *Keeping pets*
- *Outdoor pursuits*

17 Now choose your own topic for a speech, one which you might wish to use in the exam or for coursework.

a List the points you need to research.
b Indicate where you think you can find the information.
c Prepare your opening statement on the topic. It should be one medium-size paragraph (about 70 words) which attracts interest.

▼ *Exam tip!*

Be personal and passionate about your topic, as well as informative. Remember that the examiner may know nothing about the subject, so don't assume too much or use too many technical words. Humour, sparingly and appropriately used, can contribute to an enjoyable and successful presentation, as can a 'limited quantity of illustrative material'.

18 With your partner, take turns delivering your opening statements on your chosen topics. Afterwards, help each other to improve delivery and raise the level of interest in the statements.

▼ *Exam tip!*

Do you have a speech habit that you aren't aware of? Do you clear your throat often, rely on using fillers (e.g. *er*, *um* or *like*), use certain words or phrases repeatedly (e.g. *you know* or *OK*) or overuse a particular adjective (e.g. *amazing*)? Ask your partner to point out any unconscious and irritating habits so that you can work on eliminating them from your speech.

19 With your partner, try to predict the responses the examiner might make to your talk. This preparation will make it less likely that you will be put off balance by an unexpected question or comment.

▼ *Exam tip!*

A Paper 6 presentation is assessed as an individual activity (Task 1). A Paper 5 presentation (Part 1) leads into a discussion with the examiner about your chosen topic (Part 2). Both are marked out of 10 and are assessed according to the same Speaking objectives.

Further practice

a   Imagine that you have been asked for advice by a friend at another school who is having difficulty in coping with Speaking and Listening tasks. How could s/he become better prepared and more confident, and achieve higher grades? List the pointers you would email to him/her.

b   Listen to someone giving a talk on television on a particular topic (e.g. sport, travel, music). What overall mark out of 10 would you award for their content, delivery, use of language devices and ability to sustain audience interest?

c   Research the topic that you chose in Exercise 17, using your lists from 17a and 17b. Prepare your cue card. Then ask someone you know to play the role of examiner so that you can practise your talk and the subsequent discussion.

▼ *Exam tip!*

The assessment criteria for the individual and paired discussion tasks make clear that for the top band the candidate must be able to

- speak clearly and fluently
- use a range of language devices
- show considerable confidence in developing ideas and dialogue
- defend points of view
- initiate new material
- show some expertise in handling the situation
- respond promptly to changes of direction
- use a flexible sentence and language style
- consider and respond to points raised
- distinguish between fact and opinion, where appropriate
- organise content
- sustain audience interest
- use English accurately and sometimes eloquently
- articulate thoughts and feelings
- select an appropriate register
- listen to and respond to others

Part 2 | Work: information, education, employment

Unit 5: Reading

This unit focuses on selecting and organising material for the questions in the Reading paper, and on expressing responses in various styles.

❶ Read the newspaper article opposite to get the gist: Who? What? When? Where? Why? How?

❷ You may not be familiar with some of the words in the article.

    a With your partner, discuss the probable meaning of each word in the list below, after looking at it again in its context in the article.

    b Draw lines to connect words with their definitions.

    c Add the words which you consider useful to your personal vocabulary list.

definitive	selection, range, display
browse	ability to see commercial opportunities
legislation	basic requirements, essentials
array	read in an unsystematic way
potential	decisive, unconditional, final
entrepreneurialism	unstable
volatile	laws
fundamentals	possibilities

❸ Now read the article again, highlighting the main facts – e.g. *18-year-old* and *using computers at the age of two.*

❹ Copy the grid below and transfer your highlighted material from the article into the appropriate boxes. As you transfer the material, change it into your own words and reduce it.

Tom Hadfield	
The websites	
Site users	
World Economic Forum	

Internet teenage future global leader

An 18-year-old computer whiz-kid from the United Kingdom has been named as one of the World Economic Forum's 100 global leaders of tomorrow.

Tom Hadfield, co-founder of the websites Soccernet and Schoolsnet, is already a millionaire. He began using computers at the age of two and founded the soccer site when he was 12, developing it with his father Greg into one of the most popular on the Internet.

Disney

During the 1998 World Cup, up to 300,000 people visited the site at www.soccernet.com every day. The Hadfields sold 60% of Soccernet to Disney in 1999 for £15m and followed that with the establishment of Schoolsnet, now one of the largest UK education websites.

The site at www.schoolsnet.com provides educational content for teachers, parents and students and acts as a resource for students who are applying for entrance to colleges. Main features of the site include:

- School guide – a definitive illustrated guide to every school in the UK, including examination results, inspection reports and background details.
- Library – where the user can browse and buy more than 20,000 titles.
- News – an exclusive non-stop news service, reporting on all the big education stories all year round.
- Sport – Schoolsnet sponsors the English Schools Football Association, hosting and maintaining its official website (at www.esfa.co.uk) and covers school sports at all levels.
- Web guide – a unique service where the user can pick a subject and the Schoolsnet team of experts rate the best relevant education sites on the web.
- Lessons and revision – consists of interactive lessons, homework and project ideas, revision guides and tips on how to study.
- Staff room – information on legal issues, sources of funding for schools and changes in education legislation.
- Shop – an online store with an array of school-related products.

When asked how he managed to set up both websites at such an early age, Tom says: 'It just happened – neither of the companies was planned. When I was 12, I was putting football scores on the Internet as a hobby and as it happened this turned out to have commercial potential.

'Both my dad and I have had to learn as we go along since neither of us has any experience setting up businesses.'

Global leader

Hadfield is among 11 Britons under the age of 40 chosen as future global leaders by the World Economic Forum, an international non-profit-making foundation intended to promote entrepreneurialism.

The subjects of education and sport have been important to Tom at different stages in his life. 'As I have changed, my enthusiasm for football has shifted to education. I was using the Internet to revise and realised the pitfalls that exist in education websites. We have spent thousands of pounds on content for revision guides and we now offer the biggest supply of content for the education market.'

Is he worried that the mercurial Internet bubble could eventually burst?

'Schoolsnet is confident that the volatile market conditions aren't going to affect us, as we possess good business fundamentals,' he said.

Source: Adapted from *Cyprus Weekly*, 6 April 2001

5 With your partner, script a question-and-answer interview between Tom Hadfield and a young person who wants to set up a successful Internet company. What questions could be asked in order to receive the answers in your boxes in Exercise 4? Write about one side. Begin with the interviewer asking: *How do you feel about being named a global leader of tomorrow?* Put the name of each speaker in the margin – inverted commas are not required in a script. Perform the interview for the rest of your class, taking one role each.

> ▼ *Exam tip!*
>
> In the exam you will be given advice on how much to write. This tells you the length expected in order for you to earn high marks for the particular question, 'allowing for the size of your handwriting'. Do not waste time counting words; the average number of words per line on an A4 exam-booklet page is 9. For Paper 2 question 1 you are expected to write $1\frac{1}{2}$ to 2 sides.

6 The following article about higher education in the UK was published in a newspaper in Cyprus.

It's 'make your mind up' time

When you enter the Education Fair, you'll be met by a huge array of kiosks, each containing university representatives who will try to convince you that theirs is the place for you.

It is therefore best to have some idea of what you want before you go, otherwise you'll only emerge totally bewildered and clutching a heavy pile of prospectuses – only some of which you will examine in detail.

So do your homework first: arrive at the Fair forearmed with a checklist of questions you want to ask. Something along the lines of:

What do I want to study?

This is a question only you can answer, of course. If you have no idea at all of what might be suitable for you, a visit to the Fair could well make up your mind. But it is of course better to arrive with some idea of how you intend to spend the rest of your life.

Most universities offer a wide variety of courses from languages to business studies, computing and engineering. But if your aim is to go for the professions such as medicine or dentistry, then your choice will be more limited.

Look at the prospectuses and try to get some idea of the universities which offer particular degrees. It is always best to have a choice.

- Does the university have a good record in dealing with students from overseas?
- Does it have a special office to cater for the specialised needs of international students?
- Does it have many international students there already, and if so, how many?
- What support would there be, should things start to go wrong?
- Does it have a student counselling service?
- Is there an established student community from your country there already?

How much is it all going to cost?

Prices might vary considerably. Some degree programmes cost considerably more than others – for example, laboratory-based courses such as medicine, veterinary medicine and dentistry will normally cost more than non-lab degrees.

But it's not just the course fees you and your parents need to budget for on a yearly basis. You also have to think about all the other things that will eat into your cash. You will have to exist as well. You therefore also have to budget for:

- Accommodation
- Food
- Transport (how much will it cost to get from your lodgings to the campus, for example?)
- Clothing
- Entertainment

As a general rule, London and the southeast of England (Kent, Essex) are more expensive than other parts of Britain. But of course London has much to offer in terms of entertainment and sightseeing.

When thinking about cost, it is important to ask the representative of a prospective university how much you should expect to pay a year in living costs.

How will I know how good the degree is?

This is probably a better question to ask than which is the best university.

The reason for this is that many of the 'new' universities (since 1992) have been specialists in their chosen fields.

For example, many of the pre-1992 polytechnics were way ahead of the 'old' universities in Art and Design courses.

The reverse is true for subjects like medicine, dentistry and veterinary medicine – fields in which the old universities have been unchallenged and unrivalled.

So before you make your mind up, here are a few more questions to ask:
- How many of the graduates get jobs?
- Is any work experience built in to the degree?
- How well qualified are the staff? Do they do any research? Do they actually practise what they teach?
- What do employers think of the degree, and what do current students think of it?
- Would you maybe know someone from your country who is studying there?

Surprising though it may seem, many people make up their minds on the basis of people they know who have studied at a particular university.

Personal recommendation counts for a lot, and if you know someone who's already taking a course that you think you might enjoy, it's well worth your while getting in touch with them.

The sort of information they can give you will not be found in the university's prospectus.

What else is there to think about?

Taking a degree is primarily about education. But it's not all work and no play. What happens outside the lecture theatre is also important. For example:
- Does the university regularly get lots of visiting bands?
- Is it on the rail network, and therefore easy to get to other places?
- Is the university town good for shopping?
- Is it a nice place, with friendly people?

Basically, there's so much to think about that you may end up being slightly confused, possibly even suffering from an acute case of information overload. But the important thing is to take your time: don't jump at the first offer that comes your way, for others are sure to follow.

Source: Adapted from *Cyprus Mail*, 12–14 March 1999

a   Skim the article and then give it a new headline, of no more than six words, without repeating any of the words already used.

b   Scan the four sets of bullet points. For each set, write one or two sentences which include all the information/questions in a more concise (shorter) form.

c   Scan the unbulleted text. Highlight the material which gives advice. Make two columns as shown below and fill them with short phrases, using your own words as far as possible. Examples have been provided.

Do	Don't
have some idea of what you are looking for	*collect too many prospectuses*

Culture shock of new campus life

EVEN international students whose first language is English can find themselves struggling to understand an alien academic culture. The problems are very familiar to Maggie Ward Goodbody, out-going chair of the British Association of Lecturers in English for Academic Purposes. 'Students' first problems are often with listening skills,' she explains.

'They may feel nervous about this and it is certainly a steep learning curve. They need structured listening experience, for instance how to pick out the main ideas. They also need help with academic reading – how to approach an article or book, how to skim read and make notes.'

However, as students' confidence in listening skills grows, it is in the area of academic writing where more serious cultural differences become apparent. Much of British education is based on essay writing, but this may be a demanding task for students from other cultures. Suddenly they are faced with the need to express their own ideas, develop their opinions and evaluate different issues, all in polished English.

Yet for some, the concept of originating this kind of written discourse can prove problematic, and they may find themselves scoring low marks because of plagiarism, or reproducing someone else's ideas. In Britain plagiarism is regarded as academic theft, though this is not always the case in other countries. Students are expected to do research in a library before tackling an assignment, and simply regurgitating lecture notes is also not acceptable.

The best way to overcome these hurdles is to be prepared. The first step is to take a test to assess the English language skills needed to cope with the issues of academic culture.

If an accredited test indicates that a student's language skills are not sufficient to embark on a university degree, the next step is to consider pre-sessional courses, generally at the university where the student will take a degree. These can last from three weeks to an academic year, so it is wise for students to be realistic about their needs. It is generally accepted that approximately 200 hours of study are needed to improve by one band-score on some tests.

Some of the 'new' universities – those formed from polytechnics in 1992 – are experimenting with new styles of pre-sessional and foundation courses. Elspeth Jones, director of the Centre for Language Study at Leeds Metropolitan University, explains: 'Our courses are monthly, and so students from parts of the world with a different academic year can enrol at any time.'

She feels that language training in new universities is generally more flexible than in older institutions. 'Universities like ours can take students with lower language test grades and can put them through a programme that will bring them up to the required standard – though we cannot guarantee how long it will take.'

Source: Adapted from *Guardian Weekly*, 13–19 April 2000

7 Skim the article opposite for gist.

8 Underline words in the article whose meaning you are not sure of. With your partner, discuss the words, guess their meanings, look them up in a dictionary and add them to your personal vocabulary list.

9 Scan the article again, highlighting in two colours the problems which students face and the solutions to those problems.

    a   Compare your choices with your partner's and try to agree.

    b   Transfer your selected material to a grid like the one below. Rephrase as much as possible into your own words and reduce phrases and sentences to brief notes. Examples have been provided.

Problem	Solution
listening skills	*structured listening experience*

    c   Group the points logically, using arrows and brackets to show that related ideas go together.

10 List the 10 words or phrases from the article which convey the shock and difficulty experienced by the international student arriving at a British university.

11 Use ideas from the articles in Exercises 6 and 7 to complete the following task:

Two students are discussing whether or not they wish to pursue higher education in the UK. Student A is enthusiastic about the benefits; student B is concerned about the difficulties.

Write what each of them would say in the form of a dialogue set out as a script. You may add **inferences** of your own. Write about a side and a half.

> ▼ *Exam tip!*
>
> For Paper 2 question 1 you are expected to draw and develop ideas from the passage and support them with textual details. This means that you may make claims which are not directly stated in the passage, provided that they can be inferred and are relevant. Straying too far from the text will be penalised.

12 The recipe for making a chocolate cake on page 42 has been jumbled up so that the instructions are in the wrong order. Put a number next to each instruction to show the correct sequence.

Exam tip! See next page ▶

- Pour the mixture into the prepared tin and bake on the middle shelf of the oven for 30–35 minutes.
- Separate the yolks of five eggs from their whites and tip the yolks into a mixing bowl; put the whites into another bowl that is big enough to whisk them in.
- Place a heatproof bowl over a pan of simmering water. The water should be shallow and the bowl should be large enough to form a seal with the pan rim.
- Using a whisk, beat the yolks with 60 g of sugar and 60 g of self-raising flour until pale and creamy. Then beat the chocolate and butter mixture into the egg-yolk mixture. Beat the egg whites until they form soft peaks, then fold these into the chocolate mixture.
- Lightly grease the inside of a 20 cm tin with butter, then cut a strip of greaseproof paper that will wrap right around the inside of the tin. Next, cut a circle to fit the base.
- Test to see if it is cooked by sticking a skewer through the centre. Once cooked, leave to cool completely in the tin before serving.
- Break up the dark chocolate, place in the bowl and melt, then stir in thoroughly 60 g of butter and remove the bowl from the pan.
- Preheat the oven to 180° C or Gas Mark 4.

▼ *Exam tip!*

After selecting relevant material and changing it into your own words, you need to group it and order it so that your response has a logical structure, especially if it concerns a process or experience which follows set stages. The logical order is not always the order in which the text presents the material.

---

13 Read the news article opposite about an unusual restaurant in Berlin.

14 Imagine that you have booked a 'Blind Date Dinner' for you and a friend. Continue the following list of notes to be e-mailed to your friend to explain what s/he can expect to happen, in chronological order.

- *Drinks will be served.*
- *The doors will be locked.*

15 Look again at the article. The paragraphs are unusually short. Why do you think this is? Which paragraphs would you join together if this were not journalistic writing? Discuss with your partner, and then link the material into six or seven paragraphs, using this symbol: {

Berliners flock to sample true 'blind' date

Berlin, March 13 (Reuters) – The shutters are down. The curtains are drawn. The 'Last Supper' restaurant looks closed.

But diners are streaming in. They take their seats at tables decked with dark cloths. Black-clad waiters scurry to bring them their drinks. The doors are locked. Then the lights go out.

This is no wake, no power cut. It is the latest experiment on Berlin's wacky restaurant scene – dubbed the 'Blind Date Dinner' by proprietor Udo Einenkel.

Once the lights are dimmed, dinner is served. Guests cannot even see the plate in front of them, let alone their neighbour.

After a few shrieks and nervous laughter as eyes adjust to the darkness, the participants dig into their starters. Diners try to guess what they are eating.

Most start out cautiously, stabbing randomly at their plates with their forks, often coming up with nothing.

Then they throw caution to the wind. Infra-red camera footage of the event shows well-dressed businessmen eating with their hands; others scoop up left-over sauce with their fingers and even pick up their plates and lap them like cats.

'I want people to have fun and to focus on the taste,' said Einenkel. 'It is amazing how intense taste can be. You chew more slowly. You have to eat much more carefully, a bit like a blind person,' he said.

'We design our food very carefully, choosing crisp vegetables and fresh flavours that explode in the mouth. But we don't serve soup. That is too risky.'

By dessert, ice cream with some mystery fruit, the guests have become professionals at eating in the dark. Conversation has moved away from the novelty of the event and back to more normal topics – the latest film, family gossip.

The last plates are removed silently and a firefly seems to hover through the restaurant. But it is just a waiter with a stick of pungent incense.

There are audible sighs of disappointment as a waitress enters with a tray of candles. Einenkel hands out envelopes containing the menu and the chef brings round plates of the three courses to show the curious diners what they have eaten.

At €31.50 a head, the 'Blind Date Dinner' is not cheap by Berlin standards, but Einenkel says he is booked up for at least the next month.

Source: *Cyprus Review*, 13 March 2001 © Reuters Limited 2001 (adapted)

16 Underline the five words or phrases in the article which indicate the progressive change of feelings or attitudes of the diners.

17 Using ideas from the article, add two sentences to the end which explain the popularity of the restaurant. Begin *He believes that the restaurant is popular because…*

18 Using the map on page 44, take turns with your partner to explain to a visitor to the town how to get from

   a the Central Post Office to the School
   b the Town Hall to Hotel 5
   c the School to the Tourist Information Office
   d Hotel 6 to the Municipal Gardens
   e the Public Library to Eliot Street
   f Hotel 5 to Hotel 6

Exam tip! See next page ▶

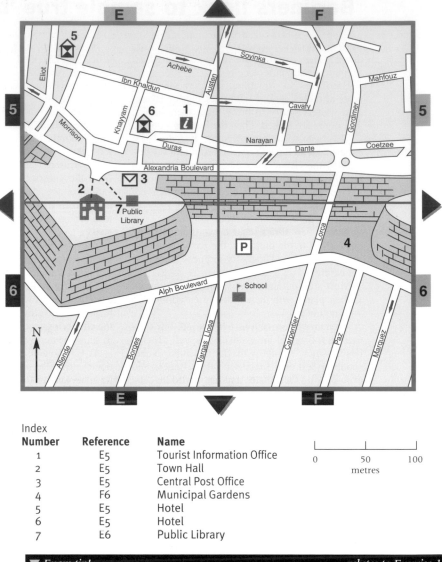

Index

Number	Reference	Name
1	E5	Tourist Information Office
2	E5	Town Hall
3	E5	Central Post Office
4	F6	Municipal Gardens
5	E5	Hotel
6	E5	Hotel
7	E6	Public Library

0   50   100
metres

▼ *Exam tip!*   *relates to Exercise 18*

When you explain a process to someone, it is important to be factually accurate, to use clear, concise expressions, and to get the instructions in the right order. Do not confuse the reader with unnecessary information. Use imperative verbs and time adverbials, e.g. *Next*, *Once*, *Then*.

Further practice

a   Write clear, concise and numbered instructions for how to tie a shoelace, put on a tie or send a text message. Next lesson, someone will try to follow your instructions exactly! See the recipe in Exercise 12 for the appropriate style.

b Think of a film you have seen recently at the cinema or on video or television. Write a one-paragraph summary of the plot, mentioning only the main aspects of the action, in chronological order, and grouping the information in complex sentences; for example, *After a plane crash in a terrible storm, an American businessman finds himself alone on a desert island, which seems…*

c Look at the labelled picture of a pair of jeans. Using the facts given as notes, which need to be grouped and ordered, write a side under the title *There's more to a pair of jeans than you thought.* You may add comments and draw conclusions from the information.

Sold at Cromwell's Madhouse, Ipswich, £19.95

Zip teeth made in Japan

Brass rivets made from Namibian copper and Australian zinc

Thread from Lisnaskea, Northern Ireland

Sewn by Fjallah Dousab, 21, in Ras Jebel, Tunisia, for 58p an hour

Cotton from Benin, where pickers earn 60p a day

Stone-washed using pumice from a Turkish volcano

Dyed in Milan using synthetic German indigo

Source: 'There's more to a pair of jeans than you thought', Fran Abrams, *Guardian Europe, G2*, 29 May 2001

Unit 6: *Directed writing*

This unit concentrates on the selection and transformation of information for Directed writing questions, and looks at newspaper reports.

1 Imagine that your school needs a new prospectus. You are one of a committee of students asked by your headteacher to collect information about how to produce a new prospectus, and you have found the leaflet opposite.

   a Form groups of three or four. Skim through the advice in the leaflet.

   b Choose one or two sections each (so that between you all seven are covered) and scan your chosen sections, underlining the essential ideas in each.

   c Take turns to tell the rest of your group what you have underlined and why. When you all agree on what to select in each section, highlight the material.

   d Use the highlighted material to write your own report for the headteacher. Write about one and a half sides, changing the wording from the leaflet. Your report should comment on

     • the purpose and aims of a school prospectus
     • the things to be considered when preparing one

Exam tip! See page 48 ▶

How to produce a good school prospectus

I Your Unique Selling Points

Most schools are in favour of the highest possible standards and responsible behaviour. So what is different about your school? What are your unique selling points?

The answers to that tell you what you need to highlight in your prospectus. That means:

- Putting it up front – ways of emphasising what you stand for include school mottoes, mission statements, headlines or quotes in larger type
- Showing these are the priorities of the head and governors
- Showing they are backed by the staff
- Illustrating what they mean in practice:
  What emphasis is given to pupils' personal, social and physical development? How does the school help children cope with the challenges of growing up?
- List extra-curricular activities
- Links with the community
- Links with local industries
- Press cuttings of school achievements

II Character

It is often easy for the real character of a school to become lost in facts and results. It is arguably one of the most important factors for parents when choosing a school. Points to emphasise include:

- Charismatic personalities within the school
- Local events for which the school is traditionally known and which involve the community, such as an annual school play, fete, or concert
- Fun events within the school which encourage team work across the age groups, such as fund-raising ideas
- Remember how influential pupils are when choosing their school

III Tone & Style

You know best who your target audience is. But remember they are not necessarily high-powered business people.

- A conversational style is probably most effective, written in plain language
- Be friendly and informative to echo how parents would be introduced to a school in person
- Avoid jargon and 'teacher-talk'
- Efficient proofreading and spell-checking are needed if you want to give a good impression about standards and attention to detail

IV Academic achievements

Year-on-year improvements are a tangible way to illustrate progress.

- Examine and build on your strongest academic areas
- Stress subjects which are not widely available in other schools
- Mention staff who have a particularly strong or interesting background
- Pupils who have achieved a personal best represent a real achievement and make good case studies

- Give details of prizes or awards to show recognition beyond external exams
- Outline your curriculum

V Facilities

Parents can be interested in all facilities, not just the state-of-the-art computer centre.

- What facilities are there for Science, Music, Drama and Sport?
- Are new facilities planned or under construction?
- Art departments and exhibitions – do they involve parents and the local community?
- Do partnerships with other schools offer additional facilities and opportunities?
- Are there information facilities such as computer Internet training, a well-stocked library or IT centre?

VI Pupil Care

Parents need to be reassured that their children will be cared for during the hours of the school day.

- How are parents involved in their child's schooling?
- What arrangements are there for parents and teachers to meet and discuss a child's progress?
- Are there any child care arrangements before or after school hours?
- Think about security – how do you ensure pupils stay in and undesirables are kept out of the school?
- Are children encouraged to eat healthy food at school?
- What steps have been taken to supervise and train staff in the use of equipment?
- What transport or road crossing patrols are provided?
- What first aid and medical care does your school provide?

VII Production & Design

Use pictures and photographs. You do not need to spend a fortune to produce a good prospectus.

- Consider producing an attractive overview of the school. Use photocopied inserts to keep other information up to date
- Look outside the school for design contacts or other professional help and advice
- Try to get local advertisers or sponsors to help with funding
- Consider what would be an appropriate level of 'glossiness' – the effect should be inviting, but remember it is not a travel brochure!
- Find a balance between text and pictures, use pupils' drawings as well as photographs. Split the text up into sections for easy reference
- Don't use badly photocopied photographs. You don't need to use professional photographers. Good-quality snaps from a school event are often just as good
- Ease of reference and clarity of layout are important. Don't over design it. Keep colours simple – maybe your school colours

For Paper 3 question 1 you may be asked to write a speech, a dialogue, a letter, a report or an article using the material in the given text(s). The information must be used in a different style and structure, and tailored to the specified task and audience. You may be asked to adopt a role and 'express what is thought, felt and imagined' (W1) by the adopted persona.

❷ Read the following news report, noticing the order in which the information is given.

Rescuers find trapped student cavers alive

Eight Swiss potholers trapped in a cave in eastern France by rising water were found alive yesterday. Rescue teams were preparing to work through the night to bring them to the surface.

Known as Bief-du-Paraud, the cave, which runs for 415 yards but only about 20 feet below the surface, is normally considered a beginner-level site for potholers.

The expedition had been part of a project for the students to develop their ability to face challenges.

Inexperienced, poorly equipped and with one of the group being partially blind, the students were initially given little chance of survival.

The potholers had entered the long narrow cave on Wednesday despite warnings from local people to stay away because rain in recent weeks had made the area dangerous.

Hope for the survival of the three women and five men – students and a teacher in their twenties – had been fading when they were found before midday by a diver who swam through a narrow passage to reach a chimney where they had taken refuge.

The diver discovered them crouched in the corridor above the water level 75 yards into the cave at Goumois in the Doubs département, 30 miles from the Swiss border. They had been trapped there for nearly 40 hours by sudden flooding on Wednesday.

Distraught relatives who had gathered at the site gave a cheer when news of their discovery was announced. The group was expected to be brought out through a hole being drilled into the chimney where they had taken refuge.

Rescuers were pumping water from the cave to avert flood danger from heavy rains over the past 24 hours. Two divers, one of whom is a doctor, were spending the night with the students in the chimney. They brought them food and water and a heating appliance.

'The group took refuge in a dry spot in a chimney,' Eric Zipper, technical adviser to the Upper Rhine cave rescue service, said. 'They are in good shape considering their ordeal. They are hungry and a little weak. They have very little food left, but they are in good spirits. There was no panic. They had a little light because they had rationed their batteries.'

Local potholing experts described the expedition as foolhardy, given the dangerous prevailing conditions. 'They were equipped only with walking shoes, jeans and anoraks,' M. Zipper said.

Markus Braendle, director of the Social Workers College of Zurich, where most of the students come from, said: 'I am so happy this nightmare is over.'

The French authorities are expected to start a legal inquiry into the conduct of the group's leader, a normal practice in such incidents.

Source: Adapted from *The Times*, 19 May 2001

❸ With your partner, look again at the report and label each paragraph with a letter according to the following key:

a   responses of participants or witnesses
b   speculation about future developments
c   facts about what happened
d   expansion and background details of story
e   official statements by the authorities involved
f   description of what is happening now

> **▼ *Exam tip!***
>
> Unlike other accounts of events, which are usually chronological, news reports generally follow this order:
>
> 1 summary of recent event
> 2 background leading to event
> 3 return to immediate situation
> 4 response of those involved
> 5 look ahead to near future
>
> The first few sentences answer the questions: *Who? What? When? Where?* and *How?*, followed by *Why?* Reporting does not include the emotional response or personal views of the reporter, or any direct address to the reader.

❹ The headline of the report in Exercise 2 is typical of newspaper reports. Look at it again, and then at the following examples. With your partner, discuss and list the common characteristics of headlines.

- **Dingo kills child on beach**
- **Riot halts match – 23 injured**
- **Scandal rocks paradise island**
- **Blind mountaineer conquers Everest**
- **Time runs out for watchmaker**
- **Stock market plunges after shame shock**
- **Talented teenager to tout for trade**

> **▼ *Exam tip!***
>
> Headlines are a kind of summary in note form, leaving out unnecessary words. Their aim is to attract reader interest in the minimum amount of space and indicate the attitude the report will adopt. Headlines tend to
> - consist of a maximum of six words
> - contain sensational vocabulary (e.g. *crash, tragic*)
> - use short words (usually no longer than two syllables)
> - use the shortest synonym (e.g. *weds* for *marries*)
> - use the present tense for recent past
> - leave out definite and indefinite articles (i.e. *the* and *a*)
>
> In headlines future events are often indicated by the infinitive, as in *Minister to resign*, and the passive is expressed by the past participle only, as in *Baby eaten by crocodile*.

5 Headlines are sometimes difficult to understand, because their grammar is so reduced. With your partner, answer these two questions for each of the following (real) headlines:

a What does it mean?

b How can you make the meaning clearer? Use more words if necessary, or change the word order or punctuation.

    i **17 aliens held**

    ii **500-year-old child found**

    iii **Squad helps dog bite victim**

    iv **Miners refuse to work after death**

    v **Wage rise bid defies ban**

6 Popular newspapers like to use the following devices in their headlines:

• puns	**Japanese yen for success**
• **assonance**	**Hit list twist**
• **alliteration**	**Fears of free fall**
• quotations	**For richer, for poorer**
• misquotations	**To buy or not to buy?**

With your partner, make up examples or find some in newspapers of each kind of word play.

7 The paragraphs in the report below – notice the headline – have been jumbled. With your partner, sequence it according to the usual structure of a news report, by putting numbers against each paragraph.

Itsy bitsy spider ... French 'spiderman' climbs Paris skyscraper

Robert, who has gained fame – and notoriety – for scaling some of the world's tallest skyscrapers without permission, climbed the 627-foot-tall TotalFinaElf building in Paris before being apprehended by the city police.

Robert says he intends to continue his career of conquering the world's highest office blocks.

Daredevil French climber and urban sherpa Alain Robert added one of France's tallest office towers to his tally on Tuesday before scaling back down into the arms of the waiting police.

The crowd which gathered to watch the man, who is sometimes called the French Daddy-long-legs, may have unwittingly tipped off police to what was going on.

Although Robert has courted arrest several times in the course of his urban climbing career, the French police are known to be a lot more sympathetic towards the local Spiderman than police in many other parts of the world.

'It was a little more difficult than I'd expected because of the wind, because of the sun,' Robert told Reuters after his <u>vertiginous</u> conquest. 'Sometimes it was a bit slippery,' he said, adding that the windows had just been washed.

Using his bare hands and <u>dispensing</u> with safety lines, Robert took about 90 minutes to reach the top of the headquarters of the oil corporation TotalFinaElf in the city's crowded La Défense business district.

Robert was apprehended on Tuesday, but not charged. According to local media reports, the police even offered him orange juice.

The law has not always been so good to Robert. In March, Chinese authorities denied him permission to climb the 88-storey Jinmau building in Shanghai.

In November last year, Singapore's police arrested Robert for attempting to scale the 920-foot Overseas Union Bank tower. And in April 1998, Parisian police arrested the stuntman after he <u>scampered</u> up the Egyptian obelisk in the Place de la Concorde and cheekily made a call on his cell phone from the top.

A mountaineer by training, Robert's first urban <u>feat</u> took place in his hometown of Valence, when the then-12-year-old scampered up to enter his family's eighth-floor apartment after losing his keys.

Now 39, his conquests have included the Sears Towers, the Empire State building, the Eiffel Tower and the world's highest skyscraper in Kuala Lumpur, Malaysia.

Source: Adapted from http://www.abcnews.go.com

8 With your partner, discuss the likely meanings of the 12 underlined words and phrases in the report. If necessary, use a dictionary to check your definitions. Add new words to your personal vocabulary list.

9 Give the report an alternative headline and a sub-heading.

> ▼ *Exam tip!*
>
> A sub-heading in the middle of a news report is a one-word or short-phrase summary – often a quotation – of the next section of the report. It signals a change of direction, prepares the reader for what will follow and entices the reader into reading on. It also breaks up the text to make it seem more accessible.

10 Look at the 'most wanted fugitive' poster on page 52.

11 Work with your partner on the following tasks, both of you making notes. Use the material given, but also make inferences.

    a Highlight the information in the poster that you would use as a journalist writing a news report about Gladwin's escape.

    b Provide likely extra details about the fugitive, such as his family background, education, general state of mind.

    c Fill in the possible details of his escape: Where? From whom? When? How?

    d Imagine how he committed his original crime of murder, and why.

    e Think of three different headlines for a report on the escape.

12 List all the alternatives to the verb *said* that can be used in news reports. Refer to the reports in Exercises 2 and 7 for help.

UNLAWFUL FLIGHT TO AVOID CONFINEMENT – MURDER, ESCAPE

JOHN STUART GLADWIN

Aliases: Michael Carerra, Miguel Carerra, Michael Carmen, John Gladwin, John S. Gladwin, Dennis H. McWilliams and Dennis Harold McWilliams.

DESCRIPTION

Date of birth: June 26, 1958
Place of birth: Miami, Florida
Nationality: American
Height: 6'0"
Weight: 170 pounds
Build: Medium

Sex: Male
Hair: Black
Eyes: Green
Complexion: Medium
Scars and marks: None
Occupation: Construction worker

CAUTION

JOHN STUART GLADWIN, WHO IS BEING SOUGHT AS A PRISON ESCAPEE, WAS AT THE TIME OF HIS ESCAPE SERVING A LENGTHY SENTENCE FOR MURDER. HE IS BELIEVED TO BE ARMED WITH HANDGUNS AND A 9 MILLIMETER RIFLE. HE MAY BE A DRUG USER.

CONSIDERED ARMED AND EXTREMELY DANGEROUS AND AN ESCAPE RISK. IF YOU HAVE ANY INFORMATION CONCERNING THIS PERSON, PLEASE CONTACT YOUR LOCAL LAW ENFORCEMENT OFFICIAL.

REWARD

A **$50,000** reward is being offered for information leading directly to the re-arrest of John Stuart Gladwin.

⓭ Scan the following passage. Then list adjective 'strings', separated by commas, to fill in the 15 gaps. Hyphenated adjectives are allowed – and encouraged! (Journalists use them as a space-saving device.) For example, gap 5 could be filled by *home-made, comic, carnival-type.*

Two (1) robbers failed in their (2) attempt to stage a (3) robbery at a (4) bank on Tuesday. Wearing (5) masks and waving (6) pistols, they threatened (7) bank staff. Tellers handed over (8) money but one (9) robber dropped the (10) bag. Cursing, he tried to pick up the (11) money but tore off the (12) mask when he could not see. (13) staff watched the (14) police escort the (15) robbers away.

⓮ Turn the following set of reporter's notes, taken at a murder trial, into a news report for a national daily newspaper, with a headline.

Durban – Feb 15 2001, 2 a.m. – woman living alone – Senne Wahl – ground floor block of flats – robbed and battered to death – only witness neighbour Lindi Madyo – 56-yr-old widow – heard disturbance – saw defendant throw hammer and gloves in bushes – described distinctive bulging eyes – defendant Jakob Peters claimed with wife at home all evening – defendant's identical twin brother Abel stood up in court – wearing same navy suit – same eyes – witness confused – couldn't confirm identity – defendant acquitted – lack of evidence – twins left court together laughing

⓯ Now you are ready to write a response to the poster in Exercise 10. You work for a local newspaper and have been assigned to write the front-page story to be published the day after Gladwin's escape from custody took place. Using the notes you made in Exercise 11, report the information in an appropriate order and style. Give your report a headline and at least one sub-heading.

> ▼ *Exam tip!*
>
> News reports typically have the following stylistic features:
> - short sentences – **simple** or **compound** (i.e. using *and, but, so*)
> - short paragraphs – often consisting of only one sentence
> - direct speech – to give authenticity and immediacy
> - **reported speech** – introduced by a variety of verbs
> - strings of adjectives – in front of nouns to qualify them
> - sensational vocabulary – to give a sense of drama

Further practice

a   You are tired of your school uniform! Use the following notes as the basis for a letter to the headteacher, asking for changes on behalf of your fellow students. You may wish to comment on gender discrimination, outdatedness, cost, discomfort or inconsistency.

Rules for school uniform

Boys, years 7–11 (first year to fifth year): grey trousers, blue pullover, white long-sleeved shirt, school tie, grey socks, black leather shoes

Girls, years 7–11: tartan skirt, red pullover, white long-sleeve blouse, school tie, white socks, brown leather shoes

Boys, years 12 and 13 (sixth form): grey trousers, single-coloured shirt, school tie, formal jacket, grey socks, black leather shoes

Girls, years 12 and 13: skirt, white blouse, school tie, white socks, brown leather shoes

Boys PE: navy shorts, white t-shirt

Girls PE: red pleated short skirt, white t-shirt

Girls may wear stud earrings but no other jewellery; boys may not wear any jewellery (except for watches for both girls and boys).

Boys' hair must be neither too long nor too short. Girls may not dye their hair unnatural colours.

---

b   Write a conversation between yourself and a friend: you agree with the idea of a school uniform, but your friend does not. Set out your conversation in the form of a script of about one side. Use the notes on the school uniform provided above.

c   Read the news report opposite, taken from the Internet. Use the information contained in the report to compose a letter to encourage people to knit jumpers for Tasmanian penguins. Add extra information that can be inferred from the report and the picture. Begin your letter *Dear Penguin Lover...*

Penguins wear jumpers

A consignment of emergency woolly jumpers has been sent to the Australian island of Tasmania to help protect a colony of penguins from oil spills.

Hundreds of volunteers started knitting when a conservation group warned that Australia's population of fairy penguins – also known as little blue penguins – was under threat.

About 1,000 of the jumpers, which cover the penguins from neck to foot, have been specially knitted, based on a pattern provided by the Tasmanian Conservation Trust.

'They have come from everywhere, even as far away as Japan,' Trust spokeswoman Jo Castle said on Monday.

'Someone in New York asked for a pattern, but we haven't received the jumper yet,' she said.

Protection from toxins

The penguins, which are indigenous to Australia, live on a small set of islands near a shipping route and are often hit by oil slicks.

Ms Castle said the penguins were 'not very happy' about their jumpers, but they were needed for their own protection.

The jumpers stop the birds preening themselves and swallowing the toxic oil, before their feathers get washed.

A copy of the pattern has been posted on the Trust's website. Ms Castle said many of the knitters were old ladies in nursing homes.

Some of them knitted in their favourite football team colours, while others stuck to more typical penguin colours. Amongst the collection is a black-and-white tuxedo, complete with bow tie.

However, fairy penguins usually have dark blue rather than black plumage on the upper parts of their body.

The jumpers are only 40cm high to fit the tiny birds – fairy penguins are the smallest of the species.

The Trust are hoping to secure another 2,000-odd jumpers.

Source: http://www.news.bbc.co.uk

Part 2

Work: information, education, employment

Unit 7: Composition

This unit looks at the writing of factual accounts, some based on personal experience and others purely informative.

1 Think about a trip you went on with your school, either educational or for pleasure. Imagine a trip if you have not had such an experience. Answer the following questions in note form:

a   Where did you go and why?
b   How long were you away?
c   Who was in the group?
d   How did you get there?
e   What time of year was it? / What was the weather like?

> **▼ Exam tip!**
>
> First-person **informative writing** is usually more successful when based, at least loosely, on real experience. Feel free, however, to exaggerate events and circumstances to make them seem more humorous or more dramatic. The examiner will enjoy your writing more and remember it better if it stands out from other compositions or coursework with the same title.

2 Make notes, using time markers, listing the events/schedule for your trip. Here is an example:

6 a.m. Tues – breakfast in freezing cold; teacher found cockroach in cornflakes

> **▼ Exam tip!**
>
> An account presents factual information in chronological order as a sequence of events. The aim is mainly informative, but there are links with descriptive and narrative writing. *The time of my life* or *An unforgettable memory*, both typical narrative titles, ask you to give autobiographical accounts of particular hours or days in your past. Each note is the basis for a paragraph, and a change of paragraph indicates a time jump.

3 Now write your full account of the school trip for your school magazine, using the material you planned in Exercises 1 and 2. What style is appropriate for your audience?

▼ *Exam tip!*   *relates to Exercise 3*

What do we mean by style? The style of a piece of writing is determined by its
- aim – what is the purpose and mood of the writing?
- speaker/writer – what kind of person is s/he claiming to be?
- audience – what do we know about their age, interests and expectations?
- vocabulary – how formal is the situation / relationship / subject?
- tone – what voice has been adopted?
- sentence structure – are sentences simple, compound, complex or a mixture?

Avoid using *then* or *and then* when writing accounts; it's an easy habit to fall into, which becomes monotonous and annoying to the reader.

4 Read the account below of a dust storm on a sheep farm from *The Road from Coorain: An Australian Memoir*, by Jill Ker Conway.

Shortly afterwards, the first terrible dust storm arrived boiling out of the central Australian desert. One sweltering late afternoon in March, I walked out to collect wood for the stove. Glancing toward the west, I saw a terrifying sight. A vast boiling cloud was mounting in the sky, black and sulphurous yellow at the heart, varying shades of ochre red at the edges. Where I stood, the air was utterly still, but the writhing cloud was approaching silently and with great speed. Suddenly I noticed that there were no birds to be seen or heard. All had taken shelter. I called my mother. We watched helplessly. Always one for action, she turned swiftly, went indoors, and began to close windows. Outside, I collected the buckets, rakes, shovels, and other implements that could blow away or smash a window if hurled against one by the boiling wind. Within the hour, my father arrived home. He and my mother sat on the back step, not in their usual restful contemplation, but silenced instead by dread. As the winds seared our land, they took away the dry herbage, piled it against the fences, and then slowly began to silt over the debris. It was three days before we could venture out, days of almost unendurable tension. When we emerged, there were several feet of sand piled up against the windbreak to my mother's garden; the contours of new sandhills were beginning to form in places where the dust eddied and collected. As we checked the property, there were dead sheep in every paddock.

Exam tip! See page 59 ▶

5 Without looking at the text, what do you remember from it? Does your partner remember the same things? Discuss why certain words and facts stayed in your mind.

6 With your partner, divide this account into paragraphs, marking the breaks and discussing your reasons for placing them there.

7 Assume that the writer of the account began with a list of preparatory notes about the storm. What do you think was on that list? Try to reproduce it.

8 Accounts can engage the reader by the use of dramatic expression or imagery. In the account of the dust storm, find and write out some examples of the following:

 a metaphors
 b unusual vocabulary
 c words to do with pace
 d words which create atmosphere
 e short sentences used for dramatic effect

9 Read the account below. It is an Internet article about a typical wedding ceremony in the Amish community, which lives in Pennsylvania, USA.

What's an Amish wedding like?

A typical Amish wedding day begins at 4 o'clock in the morning. After all, the cows must still be milked and all the other daily farm chores need to be done. There are also many last-minute preparations to take care of before the wedding guests arrive. Helpers begin to arrive by 6:30 a.m. to take care of last-minute details. By 7:00 a.m., the people in the wedding party have usually eaten breakfast, changed into their wedding clothes, and are waiting in the kitchen to greet the guests. Some 200 to 400 relatives, friends and church members are invited to the ceremony, which is held in the bride's home.

The 'Forgeher', or ushers (usually four married couples), will make sure each guest has a place on one of the long wooden benches in the meeting or church room of the home. At 8:30 a.m., the three-hour-long service begins. The congregation will sing hymns (without instrumental accompaniment), while the minister counsels the bride and groom in another part of the house. After the minister and the young couple return to the church room, a prayer, Scripture reading and sermon take place. Typically, the sermon is a very long one.

After the sermon is concluded, the minister asks the bride and groom to step forward from their seats with the rest of the congregation. Then he questions them about their marriage to be, which is similar to taking wedding vows. The minister then blesses the couple. After the blessing, other ordained men and the fathers of the couple may give testimony about marriage to the congregation. A final prayer draws the ceremony to a close.

That's when the festivities begin. In a flurry of activity, the women rush to the kitchen to get ready to serve dinner while the men set up tables in a U-shape around the walls of the living room. A corner of the table will be reserved for the bride and groom and the bridal party. This is an honored place called the 'Eck', meaning corner. The tables are set at least twice during the meal, depending on how many guests were invited. The tables are laden with the 'roast' (roast chicken with bread stuffing), mashed potatoes, gravy, creamed celery, coleslaw, apple sauce, cherry pie, fruit salad, tapioca pudding, and bread, butter and jelly.

The bride sits on the groom's left, in the corner, the same way they will sit as man and wife in their buggy. The single women sit on the same side as the bride and the single men on that of the groom. The immediate family members sit at a long table in the kitchen, with both fathers seated at the head.

After dinner, the afternoon is spent visiting, playing games and matchmaking. Sometimes the bride will match unmarried boys and girls, who are over 16 years old, to sit together at the evening meal. The evening meal starts at 5:00 p.m. The parents of the bride and groom, and the older guests, are now seated at the main table and are the first to be served. The supper varies from the traditional noon meal. A typical menu might consist of stewed chicken, fried sweet potatoes, macaroni and cheese, peas, cold-cuts, pumpkin and lemon sponge pies, and cookies. The day usually winds to a close around 10:30 p.m.

Source: Adapted from http://www.800padutch.com

> ▼ *Exam tip!*   *relates to Exercises 4 and 9*
>
> The article in Exercise 9 is purely informative, without any personal involvement on the part of the writer. The extract from a memoir in Exercise 4 tries to entertain as well as to inform, and therefore contains narrative and descriptive features. Each, however, is a kind of account and each follows a chronological structure in giving a series of facts.

⑩ Discuss as a class the following questions about the account in Exercise 9:

    a Is it an effective/interesting piece of writing? Give evidence to support your view.

    b Does it succeed in its aim to give an informative account?

    c Who do you think the audience of this Internet text might be, and is it suitably targeted?

⑪ With your partner, look at the sentence structure in the account of the wedding. What can you say about the following?

    a type/length of most of the sentences
    b how the sentences begin
    c use of lists
    d use of numbers
    e use of time references

⑫ Write an account of an annual celebration held in your country, town/village or school. It could be a festival, national holiday or public ceremony.

First make notes of the chronological stages of the event. Then develop the notes into sentences and paragraphs.

Try to use some of the techniques referred to in Exercises 8 and 11. Write about one and a half sides.

13 Read the brief account below of the last voyage of the ship *Mary Celeste*.

In the afternoon of 5 December 1872 Captain Morehouse, master of the brig *Dei Gratia*, in mid-Atlantic en route for Gibraltar, sighted another ship. He recognised it as the brig *Mary Celeste*, commanded by his old friend Captain Briggs, which had a month earlier been loading beside the *Dei Gratia* in New York. The sea was calm, the wind northerly and the sails of the *Mary Celeste* were set. Captain Morehouse signalled but received no reply. As the two vessels drew closer, Morehouse was puzzled by the haphazard way in which the brig was moving.

Captain Morehouse sent three of his men on board to investigate. They found the ship derelict but undamaged; there was no apparent reason for the crew's evacuation. The lifeboat, captain's chronometer and all the ship's papers were missing, with the exception of the log-book, whose last entry was dated ten days previously. Otherwise everything was in good order, there were plentiful supplies and the cargo was intact.

Captain Morehouse took the *Mary Celeste* to Gibraltar as salvage, but of its master, his wife and child, and the ship's crew, no trace was ever found.

brig: two-masted sailing ship
chronometer: time-keeping instrument used for navigation by the stars
salvage: that which has been rescued from a crippled ship

14 What do you think happened aboard the *Mary Celeste*? Using your imagination to supply additional details and inferring what you can from the facts given, write an exam-length composition or coursework piece entitled *A marine mystery*.

Give the account in the role of an investigator or a survivor. Remember to plan first, and to check your work before giving it to your teacher.

▼ *Exam tip!*

Don't submit a piece of writing, in an exam or for coursework, which you have not checked first. Read through your work as if you are the reader, not the writer, to ensure the following:
• it makes sense and hangs together
• it has no grammar, punctuation or spelling slips
• the handwriting is legible
• you have not repeated ideas or over-used certain words
• you have not used unclear or clumsy expressions

Make late additions by putting an asterisk (*) within your writing and the extra sentence/paragraph at the end, or by putting a caret (^) to show that you are inserting an extra word or short phrase above the line. Cross out unwanted material with a neat, single horizontal line. Correcting fluid is not allowed.

---

15 Read the magazine feature article opposite. Exam tip! See page 62 ▶

16 With your partner, list the features of the article in two columns, as shown below. Examples have been provided.

Content	Style
meals	*first person*

A Day in the Life of Juana Oliveira

Juana Oliveira, 23, is a principal dancer with the Spanish National Ballet and the youngest ever to perform the leading role in Swan Lake. *She is single and lives in Madrid with fellow dancers.*

My alarm is set for 7.30, but sometimes I ignore it and drift back to sleep until 8.00, when my cat, Carlo, gets impatient for his breakfast and jumps on me. My breakfast consists of fruit juice, cereal and vitamin pills. I can walk to the rehearsal rooms but if it's raining or I am late, as is usually the case, I jump on a passing bus.

I get through a pair of practice shoes every two weeks, and tights don't last much longer. Class begins at 9.30 but before then we must do a fifteen-minute warm-up to avoid muscle strain. Class usually lasts about two hours and then we're free to do private practice for the rest of the day, but if there is a performance that evening, then there is another afternoon rehearsal as well. I enjoy the extra buzz of preparing for a performance and pushing my body to the limit.

I have wanted to be a ballerina since I was six years old, when my grandmother took me to see *Coppelia* on my birthday and I fell in love with the beautiful skill and grace of the dancers. It was a magic world and I cried at the end because I didn't want to go back to reality.

From then on I knew what I wanted to do and I started to keep a collection of ballet photographs and to go to every performance that it was possible to get to. I still love to watch other dancers and hope one day to go to Paris, Rome or London on a ballet tour. I started attending a specialist school in Barcelona when I was eleven. My parents thought I would become too tall for a ballerina, and they were worried that the intensive training would interfere with my academic work.

Eventually they were reassured and stopped worrying about these things, and they are very proud of me now and visit often, bringing my little sister Maria to see me perform. My grandmother was very supportive from the beginning, but unfortunately she died last year. I miss her terribly but I hear her voice in my head when I am dancing, saying, 'Come on, Juana, you know you can do it!'

There was a time when I was about fifteen when I doubted my ability and resented the fact that I couldn't lead a normal life because of the need to practise in the evenings and at weekends. My friends always seemed to be doing things I couldn't join in with and I went through a lonely period.

Fortunately, my ballet teacher had faith in me and pushed me hard to prove that I had talent which shouldn't be wasted. I shall never forget the moment when I first performed in public at the age of fourteen, and when I danced my first leading role in *The Nutcracker* at sixteen. Because of that I was offered an audition for the Spanish National Ballet, and that led to a permanent contract with them. There were forty girls at the audition, and I really didn't expect them to choose me. It was my dream come true.

At lunchtime a group of us go to a local salad bar, or buy sandwiches and fruit and have a picnic in the public gardens. Of course we have to be careful what we eat and if there's a performance in the evening we have very little. Throughout the day we nibble on nuts and dried fruit to keep our energy levels up, and we drink constantly to prevent dehydration. I think I must get through at least one and a half litres of milk per day – calcium is essential for dancers to keep their bones healthy – as well as many fruit juices and bottles of mineral water. After a performance I feel ravenously hungry and treat myself to fried potatoes and omelette when I get home, or a pizza backstage.

I unwind at the end of the day with Spanish music while I rub oil into my feet, which prevents blisters and hard skin. Carlo sits on my bed and watches me mischievously. He is just waking up as I fall asleep, after an exhausting but satisfying day.

The account in Exercise 15 covers breakfast to bedtime through a typical working day. The monologue is in the present tense and mixes information about the job with personal details to create a sense of the character's personality. As in a diary, brief descriptions, thoughts, feelings and quotations are included among the events, which are recorded in chronological order.

17 Write your own *Day in the life of…* article, of about 500 words, as a coursework piece or for exam practice. Imagine you are someone speaking to a reporter. Go through the following stages:

a Invent a fictional character who has a job which you are interested in doing yourself one day and/or which you know something about. Be original! Your character can be based on a real person. Give yourself a name, nationality, age, place to live, family situation and educational background.

b List events which make up a typical working day for your invented character.

c List characteristics which make up your identity. What are your tastes in food, clothes, transport, pets and music? What are your opinions, beliefs, memories, attitudes and ambitions? Who/what are the special people/things in your life?

d Write or word-process a draft of your article, using the style of the example and following the same chronological framework. Insert information from part c into your notes for part b.

▼ *Exam tip!*

Exercise 17 is one for which the Internet may be a useful source of information, along with magazine articles and your own knowledge of the job being described. Whatever the source, you must select and adapt information, not just 'lift' it, and change it into your own words and an appropriate style. In this case your expression can be fairly informal, as it is reflecting speech, but 'accurate and effective use of paragraphs, grammatical structures, sentences, punctuation and spelling' (W5) is still required.

18 After you have checked, improved and adjusted the length of your *Day in the life of…* draft, and shown it to your teacher for advice, write the final version.

▼ *Exam tip!*

You can improve presentation by word-processing your writing, but remember that processed writing needs checking just as carefully as handwritten work. Words can be left out or deleted in error, punctuation can be neglected, and there are mistakes which a spellcheck will not pick up (e.g. *loose* for *lose*). Thesaurus and grammar-check facilities can also be misleading. Whichever method and format you choose, coursework involves planning (producing an outline), drafting (writing a rough version), revising (altering content/structure by adding, removing or changing the order of material), editing (writing an improved version with better vocabulary and sentence structures) and correcting (proofreading for errors of spelling, punctuation and grammar).

If you are working on a computer, you can scan in a photograph of someone who looks like your fictional character. Otherwise, handwrite your text in two columns, and stick on a picture you have cut out of a magazine.

Further practice

a Read the beginning of the police witness statement below.

At 8.05 p.m. on Friday 13th November I was waiting alone for an underground train to Plaza Italia on the platform at Catedral station on my way home from evening classes in English at Premium Language School. The platform was full of people and there was a lot of noise, but I could hear...

Complete this statement, or write your own real or fictional accident or crime report for the police, using a similar style.

b Plan any or all of the following exam composition or coursework titles, listing events in chronological order and including interesting, appropriate vocabulary from your personal list:

a *A battle won*
b *My proudest day*
c *History in the making*
d *An amazing find*
e *The race*

c Look at the photograph of a train crash. Imagine you are a rescue worker (ambulance, police or fire service) at the scene. Write a report at the end of the day for your team leader, giving an account of what you saw and what you did.

Unit 8: *Speaking and listening*

This unit practises role-play dialogues and interviews as part of the Speaking and listening school-based coursework component.

▼ *Exam tip!*

Dialogue is the commonest form of spoken communication. Typical dialogues have the purpose of
- complaining (about something)   • advising (someone)
- persuading (someone to do something) • explaining (something)
- requesting (something)   • apologising (for something)

 With your partner, discuss the four cartoons below and for each picture answer these questions:

a   What place does the picture show?
b   Who is in the picture and what can we guess about them?
c   What is the situation; what has just happened?
d   What is likely to happen next?
e   What do you think the characters are thinking/feeling?

A

B

C

D

2 With your partner, discuss what the two characters in each picture could be saying to each other. Practise speaking the parts of the characters in each picture. You can be as humorous as you wish! Choose the best dialogue to perform to the rest of the class.

3 In Exercise 1 the dialogues are between strangers. Choose one of the following situations and, with your partner, conduct an imaginary phone conversation between friends. You should each speak five times, so first discuss who will start, how the dialogue will develop, and how it will conclude.

- Your friend has phoned you because s/he has lost the instructions for the English homework. Explain what was set and how to approach it.
- You think your friend is spending too much time studying and needs a break. Persuade her/him to join you and some other friends for an evening out.
- You have received a bill for a library book which you borrowed but then lent to a friend. Phone the friend to ask what has happened to the book and complain that it was not returned on time.

> ▼ *Exam tip!*
>
> The Speaking and listening activities in the exam and coursework component can be more or less formal and spontaneous. You therefore need to be able to demonstrate that you can 'Use language and register appropriate to audience and context' (S4) in a variety of situations.

4 Did you express yourself differently in Exercises 2 and 3? How does talking to a friend differ from talking to a stranger? With your partner, discuss the differences between formal and informal spoken English and complete a grid, as shown below. Examples have been provided.

Formal	Informal
more precise vocabulary	*colloquial expressions*

5 Discuss as a class whether the following situations are more formal or informal:

  a   arguing with a friend about where to go on holiday together
  b   phoning a company to ask whether any summer work placements are available
  c   asking for directions in a town you don't know
  d   reporting the loss of your luggage at an airport enquiry desk
  e   answering your front door to someone trying to sell you something
  f   explaining to your parents why you have come home much later than agreed
  g   being interviewed by a college or university
  h   asking a teacher for a homework extension
  i   exchanging family news with a cousin you haven't seen for a long time
  j   phoning in sick to your place of work
  k   arguing with a family member about a television programme
  l   conducting a market survey with a passer-by in the street

Which situations weren't you sure about and why?

6 With your partner, choose situations from the list in Exercise 5 and make them the basis for practice role plays.

> *Exam tip!*
>
> In a role-play situation you need to show that you can converse confidently and naturally in English, using a range of appropriate vocabulary and grammatical structures. You need to take into account the relationship between the speakers in terms of relative ages, official positions and whether you have met before. Generally, you will use longer words and sentences for more formal situations.

7 With your partner, choose (or your teacher will allocate) one of the following situations for an extended role play to be performed to the rest of the class and assessed for coursework.

  a   A colleague explains over the phone how to do something, and answers the queries about the process.

  b   A radio or television presenter interviews someone who has discovered or invented something, and asks what difference it will make.

  c   A prosecuting lawyer cross-examines a defendant in court.

  d   A newspaper reporter questions a victim of, or witness to, a serious crime.

  e   A headteacher asks a student why their academic performance has suddenly and drastically declined.

8 In the dialogue below and on page 68, a teenager is explaining to his parent why he is apprehensive about changing to a new school; the parent is being reassuring but firm.

a   Highlight in two different colours the facts and the opinions.
b   Discuss with your partner the statements you aren't sure about.

Parent   You'll be fine; I know you will. And the papers are signed so it's too late now.

Teenager   But I shall miss my friends and I don't know anyone at the new school. You didn't ask for my opinion about the move, even though I am the one affected by it. It's further to travel every day, among other things.

Parent	At least you've visited it and you know how to find your way around. And you said you liked your new form teacher. I think she's very friendly.
Teenager	She isn't as nice as my present form teacher, who is always cheerful and encouraging. And the classes are so much bigger. I shall feel really lost and lonely, and I don't understand why you think it's necessary for me to change at this stage in my education.
Parent	They get better exam results there, which means you can go to a good university later. I think it's time you were made to work harder.
Teenager	I already work incredibly hard and do more homework than anyone else I know. Exam results aren't that important anyway, compared to being happy and having an exciting social life. I'm fed up with grown-ups always going on about results and qualifications.
Parent	You need more competition. You are wasting your abilities at the moment. A new challenge will be good for you.
Teenager	I don't need challenging – I need more time for extra-curricular activities. I've had to give up drama club and going to the gym, even though I think being physically fit matters more than studying. I never have time to spend doing things I enjoy.
Parent	You can do sport at the weekend. Weekday evenings are for homework. You are supposed to do at least two hours a night according to the new school's prospectus.
Teenager	Two hours is too much! It doesn't leave enough time to watch television, since my bedtime is 9 p.m. And how am I supposed to read books as well, which you're always telling me to do?
Parent	You should consider yourself lucky! I didn't have a television in my bedroom when I was your age. But I suppose we could consider extending your bedtime if you stop moaning about the new school.

▼ *Exam tip!*

For Task 2 and Task 3 the candidate must show considerable confidence in developing and, wherever necessary, taking charge of the situation. Points of view will be explained, often fully, in a confident, flexible and sometimes eloquent style. Candidates must 'Understand, order and present facts, ideas and opinions' (S1) and be able to distinguish between them; they should also listen carefully, consider and respond to the points raised.

9 With your partner, write a script for a dialogue in which speaker A uses only facts and speaker B uses only opinions. Begin like this:

Speaker A: You are half an hour late and the film has already started...

10 Work with your partner. A local magazine has sent a reporter to interview a national or international celebrity who is visiting your home town. Choose anyone whom you know a little bit about, and decide which of you will play the celebrity and which the reporter. Plan and practise (but do not script) the interview in the form of a question-and-answer dialogue. Make sure that the interviewee says more than the interviewer and gives fully developed responses to the questions. Record the interview and play it to the rest of the class.

11 In groups of four to six you are going to prepare for job interview role plays. Decide which two of you will be interviewers; the rest will be applicants for the jobs. Your teacher will give each group one of the job advertisements on page 70.

You will be assessed on your speaking and listening skills throughout the activity.

Work through the following stages:

a   The interviewers consult with each other and draw up lists of qualifications and characteristics which the successful applicant for the job must have.

b   Simultaneously, the job applicants individually write application letters, using false names, to be given to the interviewers by the teacher. Applicants can make up qualifications and experience!

c   The interviewers decide on the questions to be asked at interview, who will ask which questions, and in which order.

d   At the same time, the applicants individually try to predict the questions they will be asked and prepare answers to them. They also plan questions they wish to ask the interviewers.

e   The interviewers rank the application letters (based on style and accuracy of English, and appropriateness and persuasiveness of content) and announce the order for the interviews.

f   The applicants take turns to be interviewed. The teacher and rest of the class observe and make evaluation notes.

g   The applicants reflect on the role play and individually write comments on how they think they performed personally, and on the performance of the interviewers (e.g. did the interviewers make them want the job, put them at ease, ask relevant and acceptable questions?).

DYNAMIC SALES EXECUTIVES
required for
International Conference Producers

We are looking for dynamic self-starting individuals both temporary and permanent to promote our high-profile conferences to top international executives.

Suitable candidates will need good communications skills, some knowledge of MS Office and an excellent telephone manner.

An excellent remuneration package will be offered to the right candidate.

Please write in confidence to:

The Human Resources Manager
Global Conferences
10 Loveday Street, Johannesburg

ADMINISTRATIVE ASSISTANT

General office administration:

- Computer literate with excellent knowledge of Office 2000
- Excellent written and spoken English
- Some experience with Internet programmes
- Mailshots to potential clients
- Database management
- Maintaining client relationships
- Some market research required
- Excellent telephone manner
- Enthusiastic, self-motivated, able to work independently

Please send CV with photo to:

Khalid Mahmud
Amibiostat AG
P.O. Box 1600
Abu Dhabi

Lee Shipping Company Ltd

Receptionist/ Booking Clerk

We have a vacancy for the above position to work in our prestigious offices in Singapore.

The candidate will speak and write both English and Chinese. His/her duties will be answering the telephone, taking messages, making reservations, dealing with clients both personally and by telephone, working in Microsoft Word, Excel etc., typing quotations and letters, filing etc.

Please send your CV and a photo to:

Lee Shipping Co Ltd
4545 Changi Boulevard, Singapore

Leading Travel Industry Publication...
invites applicants for the following vacancy:

Junior Designer

Responsibilities include:

- assisting in the design and layout of monthly publications
- supporting design on other marketing projects
- liaising with printers

Requirements:

- ability to be creative and work independently
- ability to work to strict deadlines
- ability to work as part of a team

Please send your CV and a letter to:

Jorge Salas
Paseo Colon 220
Buenos Aires

h   At the same time, the interviewers confer and decide whom to offer the job to and why, preparing de-briefing comments for all the applicants.

i   The applicants give their feedback comments in turn.

j   The interviewers announce their decision, giving their reasons and offering advice for the unsuccessful applicants.

k   The successful applicant says whether s/he accepts the job, giving reasons why or why not.

l   The class are invited to give their comments on the whole interview role play and to make constructive criticisms of the performances.

m   The teacher says whether s/he thinks the right outcome was achieved and comments on the Speaking and listening performances of all those involved, referring to the exam marking criteria and indicating grades.

Further practice

a   Referring to the dialogue template on page 72, write two versions of a dialogue between a teacher and an ex-student who have met in the street of their home town a year after the student left school to go to university. Version A is formal and version B is more informal. The dialogue should last three to four minutes.

b   Listen to an interview on radio or television. Evaluate the performance of both speakers by giving them a mark out of 10 for speaking and listening.

c   Prepare speeches to fill the missing parts in the dialogue below between a hotel manager and a dissatisfied guest, to be performed next lesson.

Manager Good morning! How can I be of service?

Guest

Manager I'm very sorry to hear that. What exactly is the problem?

Guest

Manager No, I'm sure that can't be the case. I think you must have misunderstood.

Guest

Manager Really? I find that very surprising, but I will look into it immediately.

Guest

Manager Of course. I will let you know as soon as I have talked to the tour company representative.

Guest

Manager I understand that you feel very strongly, but I hope that it won't come to that.

Guest

Manager I'm sure we'll be able to sort this out to your satisfaction.

Guest

Part 3 | People: society, lifestyles, relationships

Unit 9: Reading

This unit continues to practise summary technique and also focuses on collating meanings and how writers achieve effects.

1 Brainstorm as a class what you think the word *centenarian* means. Think of other words you know beginning with *cent* or ending in *arian* to help you guess.

What do you think *longevity* means in the same context?

2 Using the notes in the box below, write two paragraphs about centenarians. Think about the best way to group and then order the points.

- in the US there are roughly 50,000 (1 in 8,000)
- 90% female
- more than 90% reported good health until they reached their early 90s
- about 15% live by themselves, completely independently
- there is evidence that diet affects longevity
- fastest-growing segment of US population – increasing 8% each year (1% for other age groups)
- siblings of centenarians four times as likely to survive to age 90
- longevity believed to be connected to optimistic view of life, which reduces body stress
- female centenarians three times as likely to have had children when over age 40 as were women who lived to age 73

---

3 What do you think the word **biography** means? Break it into two parts.

   a What other words do you know containing *bio*?
   b What other words do you know containing *graph*?
   c What is an **autobiography**?

4 Read the biographical fact sheet below.

Mario Frangoulis

1967 Born in Rhodesia to Greek parents

1980 Educated at the Campion School, Athens, where he excelled at drama and took the leading role in school productions

1985 Commenced three-year professional acting course at the Guildhall School of Music and Drama in London

1988 Graduated from Guildhall; won Maria Callas Award for Opera; played part of Marius in the musical *Les Misérables* in London

1990 Studied with famous tenor Carlo Bergonzi in Italy

1991 Played role of Raul in the musical *Phantom of the Opera* in London

1993 Winner of Luciano Pavarotti International Voice Award

1996 First film-acting role in *Symposium*, filmed in England

1999 Recorded first CD, *Lover's Moon* – a worldwide success – with his long-term partner, Deborah Myers

1999 Performed in Millennium Concert at the Acropolis in Athens on New Year's Eve

2000 Played role of Tony in the musical *West Side Story* in Milan

2000 Recorded second CD, *The Acropolis Concert*

2001 Debut as classical actor in the play *The Bacchae* by Euripides

2001 Toured Europe with Moscow Opera Company singing operatic arias by Verdi

2002 CD entitled *Sometimes I Dream* released in November

2004 Opened Paralympic Games in Athens

2005 US debut concert in New York in May

5 The facts about Mario Frangoulis are already in chronological order, which is typical of biographies. Now you need to organise the facts:

a   Decide and indicate, with brackets, which facts can be grouped into the same sentences.

b   Decide and indicate, with lines and numbers, how many paragraphs to write.

6 Write a summary of the life of Mario Frangoulis up to the present, using all the information in the fact sheet.

Remember to change at least some of the phrases into your own words. Join the notes to form complex sentences and write about three-quarters of a side. For example:

His second CD was recorded in 2000, which was the same year he performed in *West Side Story* in Milan.

> **▼** *Exam tip!*
>
> Summary style means selecting all the relevant material and expressing it
> • concisely – without unnecessary words
> • without repeating ideas or words – using synonyms
> • choosing precise vocabulary – avoiding vague words
> • in formal register – without colloquialisms or abbreviations
> • in complex sentences – saving words and varying structures

7 Read the brief biography of a famous children's writer below.

ROALD DAHL was born on September 13, 1916 in Wales, the son of Norwegian immigrants. His colourful experiences as a student in boarding schools were the inspiration for his books *Boy* and *Danny Champion of the World*.

Dahl became a writer during World War II, when he recounted in a short story his adventures as a fighter pilot for the Royal Air Force. The story was bought by *The Saturday Evening Post* and a long, illustrious career was born. He travelled to East Africa, where he learnt Swahili, to Greece and the USA. While in New York he met and married in 1953 a film actress with whom he had five children. His interests were antiques, paintings and greyhounds.

After establishing himself as a writer for adults, Dahl began writing children's stories in 1960 while living in England with his family. His first two novels, *James and the Giant Peach* and *Charlie and the Chocolate Factory*, are now considered classics and both have been made into blockbuster films. He was the winner of England's two most distinguished literary awards, the Whitbread Prize and the Children's Book Award, and all of his works are perennial bestsellers. He did all his writing in a garden shed with six yellow pencils by his side.

Throughout his life, Dahl took great joy in hearing from his readers. He loved nothing more than to know he was entertaining them, as well as instilling in them a love of reading and books. Dahl once said, 'I know what children like.' His stories are proof positive that he was right. Roald Dahl passed away in Oxford, England, on November 23, 1990.

Source: http://www.roalddahl.com

8 Underline any unfamiliar words in the text. Try to guess their meanings from the context. Use a dictionary to check your guesses and add the words to your personal vocabulary list.

9 Highlight the words or phrases which show that the writer thinks that

    a   Roald Dahl's life was unusual and exciting

    b   Roald Dahl's career was successful and worthwhile

10 a   With your partner, list the facts you have learned about Roald Dahl, in chronological order.

    b   Look at the list you have made. What facts do readers appear to expect in a biography? For example: date of birth.

11 Select the key points from your list in Exercise 10a and in one complex sentence say who Roald Dahl was.

12 Now look at the four sentences below. Which one is the best in terms of content and style? Why? Do the rest of the class agree? Is your sentence better? Can you improve your sentence?

    a   Roald Dahl was born in Wales, where he wrote children's stories.
    b   After establishing himself as a writer for adults, Roald Dahl began writing children's stories in 1960, his first two being classics.
    c   Roald Dahl, who wrote children's stories with yellow pencils, was a fighter pilot during the Second World War.
    d   Roald Dahl, who was born in 1916 in Wales of Norwegian descent, was a highly successful author of prize-winning children's fiction which inspired a love of reading.

13 How many of the following connectives do you regularly use in your writing? Tick them.

when	although	so that
who	if	as if
whom	before	as though
whose	after	even if
which	since	even though
wherever	unless	in order to
while	because	in spite of
whilst	until	as well as
where	as	as soon as
whereas	for	owing to
whether	despite	because of

> ▼ *Exam tip!*
>
> The words *and*, *but* and *so* are also connectives, but they don't enable you to form complex sentences, only compound ones. Overusing them will make your writing sound repetitive, immature and imprecise. They also restrict your ability to vary your style, as they are not normally used at the beginning of sentences as other connectives can be.

⓮ Asterisk the connectives listed in Exercise 13 which you never use.
Write some sentences which show you know how to use them.

⓯ Join these three simple sentences into one complex sentence using some of the ways mentioned in the exam tip above. Experiment with changing the order of the clauses.

Roald Dahl wanted his readers to be entertained by his books.
He also wanted them to love reading.
He knew what children like.
He had five children.

⓰ Read the newspaper obituary on page 78, as published on the Internet.

⓱ Judging from the article, what is an **obituary**?

a What is its subject?   c Why would someone write one?
b When is it published?   d Why would someone read one?

⓲ Using connecting lines, match the 12 underlined words in the article with their definitions:

epitaph   group of commercial firms
foibles   chose, decided
endearing   words inscribed on a tomb
constancy   time limit
misfortune   music written for orchestra
rivalry   gathering of professional people
combat   firmness, unchangingness
syndicate   bad luck
convention   competitiveness
opted   minor weak points of character
deadline   battle or contest
symphonies   likeable

Cartoonist Charles Schulz dies at 77

PEANUTS © United Feature Syndicate, Inc.

Feb. 13, 2000

'Peanuts' creator Charles M. Schulz died on Saturday, turning his farewell note in Sunday papers into an epitaph for both a comic strip and its creator.

Schulz was 77, and died in his sleep at about 9:45 p.m. at his home in Santa Rosa, said his son, Craig. Only his wife, Jeannie, was with him when he died. Schulz was born in St. Paul, Minnesota, USA on Nov. 26, 1922.

He was diagnosed with colon cancer and suffered a series of small strokes during emergency abdominal surgery in November 1999. He announced his retirement a few weeks afterwards.

He studied art after he saw a 'Do you like to draw?' ad. His wildly popular 'Peanuts' made its debut on Oct. 2, 1950. The troubles of the 'little round-headed kid' and his pals eventually ran in more than 2,600 newspapers, reaching millions of readers in 75 countries. His last strip, appearing in Feb. 13 Sunday editions, showed Snoopy at his typewriter and other Peanuts regulars along with a 'Dear Friends' letter thanking his readers for their support.

Over the years, the Peanuts gang became a part of American popular culture, delivering gentle humor spiked with a child's-eye view of human foibles.

Sergio Aragones, a *Mad* magazine cartoonist and friend for more than 30 years, called Schulz 'a true cartoonist.' 'In a couple of centuries when people talk about American artists, he'll be the one of the very few remembered,' Aragones said. 'And when they talk about comic strips, probably his will be the only one ever mentioned.'

One of the most endearing qualities of 'Peanuts' was its constancy. The long-suffering Charlie Brown still faced misfortune with a mild 'Good grief!' Tart-tongued Lucy still handed out advice for a nickel. And Snoopy, Charlie Brown's wise-but-weird beagle, still took the occasional flight of fancy back to the skies of World War I and his rivalry with the Red Baron.

He was drafted into the Army in 1943 and sent to the European theater of war, although he saw little combat.

After the war, he did lettering for a church comic book, taught art and sold cartoons to *The Saturday Evening Post*. His first feature, 'Li'l Folks,' was developed for the *St. Paul Pioneer Press* in 1947. In 1950, it was sold to a syndicate and the name changed to 'Peanuts,' even though, he recalled later, he didn't much like the name.

Although he remained largely a private person, the strip brought Schulz international fame. He won the Reuben Award, comic art's highest honor, in 1955 and 1964. In 1978, he was named International Cartoonist of the Year, an award voted by 700 comic artists around the world. He was to have been honored with a lifetime achievement award on May 27 at the National Cartoonists Society convention in New York.

In his later years, he spent much of his time at his Redwood Empire Ice Arena in Santa Rosa, about 60 miles north of San Francisco, where he frequently played hockey or sipped coffee at the rink's Warm Puppy snack bar.

'Peanuts,' meanwhile, had remained an intensely personal effort. He had had a clause in his contract dictating the strip had to end with his death. While battling cancer, he opted to retire it right then, saying he wanted to focus on his health and family without the worry of a daily deadline.

'Why do musicians compose symphonies and poets write poems?' he once said. 'They do it because life wouldn't have any meaning for them if they didn't. That's why I draw cartoons. It's my life.'

Source: Adapted from http://www.salon.com

19 Write any words you did not know before, and their definitions, in your personal vocabulary list.

> ▼ *Exam tip!*
>
> The passage is in American English, which differs from British English somewhat in its vocabulary, tense usage and spelling; notably in words ending in *er* and *or* such as *theater* and *color*. You may use American English in the IGCSE exam, provided that you use it consistently and do not mix it with British usages and spellings.

20 Look at the prefixes in the words listed in Exercise 18: *epi-, con/com-, mis-, syn/sym-*.

   a Give examples of other words beginning with these prefixes.
   b What do you think these prefixes mean?

> ▼ *Exam tip!*
>
> The dictionary definition of **prefix** is a 'letter or group of letters added to the beginning of a word to make a new word'. Prefixes are very common in English (the word *prefix* has a prefix!), and most of them come from Latin or Greek. Knowing their meanings helps you to guess unknown vocabulary and to spell words correctly – e.g. whether it is *hyper* ('above') or *hypo* ('below'), or whether to use one *s* or two in *dissatisfied*.

21 With your partner, see how many prefixes and their meanings you can list in five minutes. It is worth looking back at Exercises 1 and 3. Your teacher will collect the results on the board.

22 The material you select for summary must relate to the exact wording of the question. Using three different colours, or a mixture of highlighting and underlining, select material in the obituary which you would use to summarise

   a Charles Schulz's life and death
   b Charles Schulz's career and reputation as a cartoonist
   c the 'Peanuts' comic strip

Compare your choices with your partner's. Are there any facts which you would use in more than one section?

23 Write a summary of the obituary, in one side, which combines the material for parts a, b and c in the previous exercise.

Remember to change the material into your own words, group it, order it, and express it in complex sentences.

24 Read the two biographical extracts (Texts A and B) on pages 80 and 81 about Rasputin, the 'mad monk' of Russia.

25 Which of these two ways of relaying similar information did you find

   a more informative? Give examples.
   b more interesting? Give reasons.

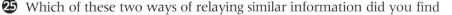

Text A
Rasputin

Gregory Rasputin was born on January 10, 1869, into a Siberian peasant household. He spent much of his early adult life wandering Russia as a monk. In 1905, after the first Russian revolution, Rasputin infiltrated the imperial inner circle as the last in a long line of mystics. His miraculous ability to stem the bleeding of their haemophiliac son

Alexei made him indispensable to the isolated, confused royal couple, Tsar Nicholas II and his wife, Alexandra. The support he provided, however, was as much emotional as practical.

Between 1905 and 1914, Rasputin charmed everyone he met, soothed the unhappy noblewomen who were his devotees and pursued an apparently sober holiness. When war arrived in 1914, the power-vacuum left by Russia's crushing defeats and Nicholas's absence at headquarters brought Rasputin almost supreme power alongside Alexandra. Monk and tsarina governed corruptly, unwisely appointing prime ministers and bishops, and even arranging the dismissal of the commander-in-chief, Grand Duke Nikolai. 'I'm a devil,' the monk admitted. 'I used to be holy.'

Everyone could see that the tsarina and the peasant-mystic Rasputin were driving Russia to ruin, hence the plot to kill him. The leader of the conspiracy was the fabulously wealthy Prince Felix Yussoupov, whose version of the events surrounding Rasputin's death was that he lured the monk to his palace, poisoned, shot and then tried to drown him, but still he would not die. What is certainly true is that when Rasputin's body was stuffed through the ice of the River Neva, he was still alive.

Source: Adapted from 'His life was cloaked in legend and myth…', *The Sunday Times*, 12 March 2000

26 Express the following quotations from Text A in your own words. You may use a dictionary or thesaurus to help you.

a *…infiltrated the imperial inner circle…*
b *…the power-vacuum left by Russia's crushing defeats…*
c *…brought Rasputin almost supreme power alongside Alexandra…*
d *…were driving Russia to ruin…*
e *…whose version of the events surrounding Rasputin's death…*

27 Re-read Text B, selecting words and phrases which convey

a violence   b drama   c suspense

Referring closely to the language used by the writer, explain in each case why your choices are effective.

> ▼ *Exam tip!*
>
> Paper 2 question 2 is a two-part question which asks you to choose and quote a range of words and phrases from specified paragraphs of the passage to illustrate each part of the question. You are required to analyse your choices to explain how they are able to convey a particular feeling or atmosphere, e.g. mystery, fear, enjoyment. In addition to unusual, striking and powerful vocabulary and imagery, you can comment on relevant grammatical or literary features, e.g. irony, repetition, contrast, incongruity (all of which occur in Text B). You should not, however, simply list grammatical or literary terms; to show your understanding of how writers achieve effects you must make clear what the writer's use of language **evokes** in the reader, and why, e.g. 'savage, inhuman cry' suggests an enraged beast.

Nicholas and Alexandra

By evening, the cellar room had been prepared. On the table the samovar smoked, surrounded by plates filled with the cakes and dainties that Rasputin liked so much. On the granite hearth a log fire crackled and scattered sparks on the hearthstones.

Doctor Lazovert put on rubber gloves and ground the cyanide of potassium crystals to powder. Then, lifting the top of each cake, he sprinkled the inside with a dose of poison which, according to him, was sufficient to kill several men instantly.

When Yussoupov went alone at midnight to Rasputin's flat, he found the monk smelling of cheap soap and dressed in his best embroidered silk blouse, black velvet trousers and shiny new boots. Yussoupov promised, as he took his victim away and led him down into the cellar, that Princess Irina was upstairs at a party but would be down shortly.

Alone in the cellar with his victim, Yussoupov nervously offered Rasputin the poisoned cakes. Rasputin refused. Then, changing his mind, he gobbled two. Yussoupov watched, expecting to see him crumple in agony, but nothing happened. Then, Rasputin asked for the wine, which had also been poisoned. He swallowed two glasses, still with no effect. Rasputin took some tea to clear his head and, while sipping it, asked Yussoupov to sing for him with his guitar. Through one song after another, the terrified murderer sang on while the happy 'corpse' sat nodding and grinning with pleasure. Huddled at the top of the stairs, scarcely daring to breathe, Purishkevich, Dmitry and the others could hear only the quavering sound of Yussoupov's singing and the indistinguishable murmur of the two voices.

After this game had gone on for two and a half hours, Yussoupov could stand it no longer. In desperation, he rushed upstairs to ask what he should do. Lazovert had no answer; his nerves had failed and he had already fainted once. Grand Duke Dmitry suggested giving up and going home. It was Purishkevich, the oldest and steadiest of the group, who kept his head and declared that Rasputin could not be allowed to leave half dead. Steeling himself, Yussoupov volunteered to return to the cellar and complete the murder. Holding Dmitry's revolver behind his back, he went back down the stairs and found Rasputin seated, breathing heavily and calling for more wine. As he did so, Yussoupov fired. The bullet plunged into the broad back. With a scream, Rasputin fell backward onto the white bearskin.

Hearing the shot, Yussoupov's friends rushed into the cellar. They found Yussoupov, revolver in hand, calmly staring down at the dying man with a look of inexpressible disgust in his eyes. Although there was not a trace of blood, Doctor Lazovert, clutching Rasputin's pulse, quickly pronounced him dead. The diagnosis was premature. A moment later, when Yussoupov, having surrendered the revolver, was temporarily alone with the 'corpse', Rasputin's face twitched and his left eye fluttered open. A few seconds later, his right eye also rolled open. Suddenly, while Yussoupov stood rooted to the floor, Rasputin, foaming at the mouth, leaped to his feet, grabbed his murderer by the throat and tore an epaulet off his shoulder. In terror, Yussoupov broke away and fled up the stairs. Behind him, clambering on all fours, roaring with fury, came Rasputin.

Purishkevich, upstairs, heard a savage, inhuman cry. It was Yussoupov: 'Purishkevich, fire, fire! He's alive! He's getting away!' Purishkevich ran to the stairs and almost collided with the frantic prince, whose eyes were bulging out of their sockets. Recovering, Purishkevich dashed outside into the courtyard. Rasputin, who half an hour before lay dying in the cellar, was running quickly across the snow-covered courtyard towards the iron gate which led to the street. In a few seconds he would reach it. Purishkevich fired. The night echoed with the shot. He missed. He fired again. Again he missed. He raged at himself. Rasputin neared the gate. Purishkevich bit with all his force the end of his left hand to force himself to concentrate and he fired a third time. The bullet hit Rasputin in the shoulders. He stopped. Purishkevich fired a fourth time and hit him probably in the head. Purishkevich ran up and kicked him as hard as he could with his boot in the temple. Rasputin fell into the snow, tried to rise, but he could only grind his teeth.

With Rasputin prostrate once again, Yussoupov reappeared and struck hysterically at the bleeding man with a rubber club. When at last the body lay still in the crimson snow, it was rolled up in a blue curtain, bound with a rope and taken to the frozen Neva where Purishkevich and Lazovert pushed it through a hole in the ice.

Three days later, when the body was found, the lungs were filled with water. Gregory Rasputin, his bloodstream filled with poison, his body punctured by bullets, had died by drowning.

Source: Adapted from Robert K. Massie, *Nicholas and Alexandra*, Atheneum, New York, 1967

28 Look at these two ways of expressing the same fact:

Text A: *What is certainly true is that when Rasputin's body was stuffed through the ice of the River Neva, he was still alive.*

Text B: *Gregory Rasputin, his bloodstream filled with poison, his body punctured by bullets, had died by drowning.*

a How do the statements differ and what is the effect of each?
b What are the aims and audiences of each text?
c Which style is more appropriate for summary and why?

29 Select material, from both extracts, which would be relevant to a summary of Rasputin divided into three paragraphs:

a his life and position
b his character and tastes
c the circumstances and causes of his death

List the points you have selected, collated, grouped according to paragraph, and changed into your own words.

> ▼ *Exam tip!*
>
> In all parts and both tiers of the Reading component of the exam you are required to 'Understand, explain and **collate implicit** meanings and attitudes' (R2) as well as 'Understand and **collate explicit** meanings' (R1). This means that you need to demonstrate comprehension of the passage(s) by responding to both their stated and implied meanings, and by indicating an awareness that language choices reveal attitudes.

30 Write a summary of Rasputin's life and death, of about one side. Use your collated notes from Exercise 29, synthesising the material.

Further practice

a Research the biography of someone who interests you and write a summary of about one side. Read it to your class next lesson, leaving out the person's name. Can your classmates guess who it is?

b Someone has been found in a coma on a park bench in a major city. The only clues to identity are the contents of the person's pockets:

- handkerchief with initial *M*
- photo of two teenagers
- bottle of pills
- set of car keys
- theatre programme
- packet of sweets
- local restaurant receipt
- wedding ring
- map of the city
- large sum in cash
- gold watch
- sunglasses

You are a police spokesperson. Write a radio bulletin about the person, who is now in intensive care in hospital, in the hope that a relative or friend will come forward to identify him/her. The statement should contain both facts and inferences. You are invited to interpret the pocket contents and to add biographical details of your own that you think are appropriate. Begin as follows:

Police are anxious to establish the identity of a person found unconscious this morning in Jubilee Park by a jogger...

c Without using any of the vocabulary in the following description of Snoopy, write a summary of his character in no more than 50 words in two sentences.

PEANUTS © United Feature Syndicate, Inc.

Snoopy is an extroverted beagle who fantasises about being a hero. He is a virtuoso at every endeavour – at least in his daydreams atop his doghouse. He regards his master, Charlie Brown, as 'that round-headed kid' who brings him his supper dish. He is fearless, though prudently cautious, about 'the cat next door'. He never speaks – that would be one human trait too many – but he manages to convey everything necessary in facial expressions and thought balloons. A one-man show with superior intelligence and vivid imagination, he has created such multiple personalities as Joe Cool, World War 1 Flying Ace, Literary Ace, Flashbeagle, Vulture, Foreign Legionnaire, etc.

People: society, lifestyles, relationships

Unit 10: *Directed writing*

This unit looks at and practises different types of persuasive writing. Further advice is given on choosing appropriate vocabulary, organising material and appealing to an audience.

1 Read the extract from a holiday brochure below.

Hotel Paloma

Tamara

Location: Situated on the unspoilt southern coast of the beautiful Pacific island of Tamara, only 20 km from the lively capital of Santa Barbara, the Paloma hotel complex is the ideal location for an exotic holiday at any time of the year.

Rooms: Recently built, this four-storey luxury hotel has 120 air-conditioned rooms, each with en suite bathroom, tv, fridge and spectacular sea or mountain views.

Facilities: In addition to the two sandy private beaches, there is a fabulous landscaped tropical garden, two swimming pools, a sauna and a casino. Sports facilities include a mini-golf course, fully equipped gym, tennis courts and snooker tables. Sailing and riding are catered for nearby.

Excellent shopping and sophisticated nightlife are available in the capital, to which the hotel provides a regular courtesy bus service. There are three ethnic food restaurants to choose from, as well as indoor and outdoor café bars and a disco. A unique feature is the floodlit grotto bar, which has live music every night.

Room service is available from friendly staff 24 hours a day.

② Underline all the adjectives in the brochure extract. Discuss the following questions with your partner:

   a What associations do the underlined words evoke?
   b Which emotions does the reader feel?
   c What kind of audience is the brochure targeting?
   d How effective is this extract as persuasive writing?

③ Imagine you recently stayed in the Hotel Paloma for a fortnight with family or friends. List a few problems, e.g.

- Were all the facilities completed and adequate?
- Were you satisfied with your room? And the noise level?
- Did the beach live up to expectation?
- How was the bus service, the room service, the service generally?
- How would you describe the catering?

Write a letter of complaint to the travel agency, Pegasus Travel, which arranged your holiday at the Hotel Paloma. Persuade the manager to give you a refund or another holiday as compensation.

Refer to claims made in the brochure and be specific about your complaints. Write about one and a half sides.

> **▼ Exam tip!**
>
> Persuasive writing is intended to convince someone to do something which is for their own benefit or that of the writer. To be effective it must be focused clearly on the purpose, give specific evidence, show awareness of the audience being targeted, and choose vocabulary to evoke the required emotional response (e.g. guilt, sympathy, fear). To be persuasive be firm but polite; extreme language or abuse can defeat your objective.

④ Read the magazine article on page 86 about the pains and pleasures of becoming a jogger.

⑤ Imagine you are the speaker in the article and you are trying to persuade a reluctant friend to join you in taking up jogging.

   a Scan the article, highlighting information which you would use to persuade your friend that jogging is a worthwhile activity.
   b Using a different colour highlighter, find points which someone would use to explain why s/he is not keen on becoming a jogger.

⑥ Using the material you selected for Exercise 5, write a one-side continuation of the following telephone conversation. Choose words which convey the appropriate attitude of enthusiasm or reluctance:

Me: I've just got back from a really good run and feel wonderful. You really ought to try jogging, you know. We could do it together.

Friend: You must be joking!...

Exam tip! See page 87 ▶

The joys of jogging

If you don't jog, jogging is impossible. When you do run for a couple of minutes – when needs really must – you find yourself beetroot in the face, slick with sweat and barely able to breathe. It is painful and undignified. And if in a two-minute dash to a bus stop you can be reduced to such a wreck, what would happen in four minutes? How can it be physically possible to run for 20, which is how long they say 'beginners' should jog for?

I jog now, very slowly, but very definitely and sort of regularly (in a random way), and I enjoy it. Or at least I feel smug and energetic and quite holy for having done it. I don't care that people tease me for shuffling along so slowly or for chatting so much while I shuffle. I am a jogging evangelist: I think it is the best exercise anyone can possibly do and I think that it has a more profound impact on your body than anything else you can do. If you want to get fit or lose weight there's nothing better.

There will always be people who preach the evils of jogging – we've all heard about dedicated joggers dropping dead at 50 – but in last week's *British Medical Journal*, Danish researchers said that their study of 20,000 people showed that regular joggers are far less likely to die prematurely than non-joggers.

So it's good for you. But how to start? I'll never forget how hard it was at the beginning: gazing up at an Everest of sweat and panting, and knowing that I would never be able to do it and that, even if I did, it would be terminally boring.

For the next three months or so, I stuck rigidly to my 'running' routine. I went to the gym three times a week, and I did my two minutes jogging, two minutes walking. … Slowly, it became easy. I stopped going red in the face and feeling uncomfortable. Then one morning a friend joined me at the gym. Not a fitness freak but an ordinary woman.

I watched her jog, next to me, for 16 minutes. When I got off, at the end of my programme, she continued for another four minutes, but said nothing.

It was time to take the next step: continuous jogging. It had to be at walking pace, clearly, but continuous. First I did four minutes, then six minutes … much duller than two minutes. It was during this period that I took the big step off the running machine and into the outside. I went for 'a run' in the park. The first thing I noticed was how much faster the time went by outside. Within a month I was going for 20-minute runs.

Enter another friend, a regular jogger. He watched me run (walking alongside me) and said that there was no point in going so slowly. And so I speeded up so that I was running, although very slowly, rather than walking. A major breakthrough.

A marathon-running friend of my mother told me not long afterwards that I was doing fine. She said not to listen too much to macho male joggers anyway: the secret was – never run at a speed that it was uncomfortable to chat at.

About eight months into my new life, I returned to the gym for my fitness test. I was weighed and found that without ever actually getting unpleasantly tired, I had lost about eight pounds. And just like that, I was, a new woman. I could run for buses without breaking into a sweat.

My love of jogging is now about three years old and prone to dips. For the past four months, I've barely been out to the park once a week. But it doesn't matter. However long I leave between runs, I can still go out and jog for 20 minutes, and feel better for it. And the best of it is that not only is jogging free, but you can do it anywhere you find yourself.

Source: Adapted from *The Guardian*, 12 September 2000

7 Your gym has asked you to produce a one-sided leaflet to hand out to its members, to explain

- the physical benefits of jogging
- the mental benefits of jogging
- the process of becoming a jogger

Write the flyer, using relevant material from the article opposite and anything else suitable which can be inferred from it. Use your own words, and organise the points under appropriate topic headings.

8 In groups of three, imagine you are a student council committee trying to raise money for a new facility for your school (e.g. a swimming pool, sports hall, computer room or theatre).

Write a joint letter to former students of your school to persuade them to donate money towards the project.

- What do you know about the audience?
- What emotions do you want them to feel towards the school?
- What would be an appropriate tone and style to use in the letter?

First plan the structure and content of your letter, making notes on what you would put into each section. Write about one and a half sides. One of you can read it out to the class, which can vote on the most persuasive letter.

9 Read the newspaper report below on childhood addiction to smoking.

Nicotine addiction can start after first few cigarettes

London (AP)

Scientists have confirmed a suspicion held by some smokers but never proven: it could take just a few cigarettes to become addicted.

Experts have tried for years to determine how long people have to smoke before becoming addicted, said Dr Richard Hurt, director of the Nicotine Dependency Unit at the Mayo Clinic.

'The best answer to date has been 1–2 years,' said Hurt. 'There's been a suspicion that many people become addicted very quickly, but this is really the first hard evidence that we've had that this occurs.'

Research reported this week in the British Medical Association journal *Tobacco Control* found that several 12- and 13-year-olds showed evidence of addiction within a few days of their first cigarette.

The study was conducted by scientists at the University of Massachusetts in 1998. The experts followed 681 teenagers between the ages of 12 and 13 from seven schools in central Massachusetts for a year and tracked their smoking habits.

Symptoms

Symptoms include cravings, needing more to get the same buzz, withdrawal symptoms when not smoking, feeling addicted to tobacco, and loss of control over the number of cigarettes smoked or the duration of smoking.

A total of 95 teens said they had started smoking occasionally – at least one cigarette a month – during the study. The scientists found that 60, or 63%, of them had one or more of the eight symptoms of addiction.

A quarter of those with symptoms got them within two weeks of starting to smoke and several said their symptoms began within a few days.

Sixty-two per cent said they had their first symptom before they began smoking every day, or that the symptoms had made them start smoking daily.

It is possible that adolescents could be more sensitive to nicotine and that addiction may take longer in people who start smoking at a later age.

'The really important implication of this study is that we have to warn kids that you can't just fool around with cigarettes or experiment with cigarettes for a few weeks and then give it up,' said Dr Joseph DiFranza, who led the research team at the University of Massachusetts. 'If you fool around with cigarettes for a few weeks, you may be addicted for life.'

Source: Adapted from *Cyprus Weekly*, 22 September 2000
Used with permission of The Associated Press. Copyright © 2000. All rights reserved.

10 Express the information in the graph below in sentences, e.g.

Girls are more likely than boys to smoke after the age of 14.

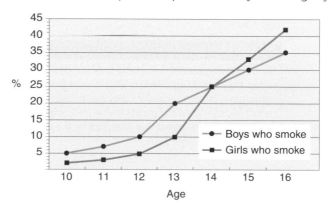

11 Write a letter to a friend or relative your own age who has just taken up smoking cigarettes, to persuade her/him to stop.

Use facts and inferred ideas from the article in Exercise 9, and also refer to the data in the graph in Exercise 10.

12 One of the most common forms of persuasive writing is advertising, as in the holiday brochure in Exercise 1. With your partner, study the claims made by these three different brands of toothpaste.

Which do you find the most persuasive and why? Can you write an ad that is even more persuasive?

a For confidence, happiness and success, you need Flossy.
b Your refreshing, bright, white smile says you are a Dentigel dazzler.
c Healthy teeth and gums can be protected by regular brushing with scientifically proven, carbofluoride-rich Toothsome toothpaste.

13 Think about the following pairs of words. For each pair, tick the word which is more powerful emotionally. Does the class agree? Discuss the reasons in each case.

a slaughter/kill
b own/possess
c house/home
d attractive/beautiful

e reluctantly/unwillingly
f love/adore
g phobia/fear
h sad/sorrowful

14 Here are two versions of a 'For Sale' advertisement for the same second-hand bicycle:

FOR SALE	For Sale
Very old, rather worn bicycle, old-fashioned style, in need of some repair, going cheap.	Characterful antique bicycle in reasonable condition available at a bargain price.

With your partner, decide which ad is more likely to be successful, and why its vocabulary is more persuasive.

Write an ad of similar length for a possession, real or imaginary, which you wish to sell. Consider carefully your choice of vocabulary, grammar and order of information.

When you have finished drafting and improving it, read it to the class. Would they want to buy your object for sale?

⑮ To avoid giving offence personally or politically, persuasive writing sometimes uses **euphemism** (more tactful and less emotive words in place of what is really meant).

With your partner

a identify and underline the euphemisms in the following sentences
b replace them with more honest phrases
c discuss the differences of effect in each case

  i She is quite well built for someone her age.
  ii The staff have voted to take industrial action.
  iii Unfortunately, there is no alternative: the dog must be put to sleep.
  iv His behaviour has become somewhat odd lately.
  v Our nation will be strengthened by ethnic cleansing.

Get into groups of three to five students for Exercises 16–26. You are going to work on a charity project.

⑯ What is a 'charity'?

a List the kinds of things which charities raise money for.
b List as many official charities as you can think of.
c Discuss why you think they need to exist.

⑰ Read the Red Cross appeal letter opposite, which was written in 1995 during the Bosnian conflict.

⑱ Underline the words/phrases in this letter which you find the most persuasive. Compare your choices with the rest of your group. Why do you think the chosen words have this effect?

> ▼ *Exam tip!*
>
> It is likely that you have underlined the battle metaphors and clichés, and the words to do with cold and misery, which are all intended to make the reader feel fear and pity. The personification of winter as a bringer of disease, starvation and death intensifies the effect of if being a greater enemy than the war. The contrast between *them* and *us*, and the emphasis on the passing of time, create a feeling of guilt and a sense of urgency. These are techniques you can use in your own persuasive writing.

⑲ What exactly is the purpose of the letter? Discuss in your group

a the kinds of material which are included
b whether the content is fact or opinion, or both
c why you think statistics and numbers are used

⑳ Think about the Red Cross name and symbol. Why are they memorable?

a Draw other charity symbols or **logos** you can think of (e.g. the candle and barbed wire for Amnesty International).
b Look back at and discuss the names you listed in Exercise 16b.
c What can you conclude about effective names and symbols?

British Red Cross

UK Office
44 Moorfields
London EC2Y 9AL
Telephone 0870 170 7000
Fax 020 7562 2000

Caught in the conflict.
Fighting to survive the winter months.
Together we can help them win.

Registered Charity No 220949

Dear Supporter,

We can't help but be moved by the pictures of human suffering in the conflict in former Yugoslavia. But it's a sad fact that this is just the tip of the iceberg. In Georgia, Azerbaijan and Afghanistan the misery of civil war victims is going almost unnoticed.

Across Eastern Europe thousands of innocent families have escaped from the fierce fighting only to face a new risk from the deadly combination of bitter cold, starvation and disease.

In the middle of winter blankets and sheeting could make the difference between life and death.

Amra's refugee family is typical of many. Since last June they have lived in a damp and unheated cellar underneath the town of Mostar. Now as winter tightens its deadly grip, her family of 13 huddle together for warmth in no more clothing than they stand up in.

But there are refugees who don't even have a roof over their heads. Many fleeing families are spending the bitter winter months in the open, in the tents of hillside refugee camps, where they must brave the snow, wind and rain in temperatures dropping as low as –25°C.

To make matters worse, disrupted food supplies often mean that people haven't eaten properly for a year or more. Many women have lost as much as 16 kg and malnutrition means children are becoming vulnerable to the slightest infection.

Homeless, hungry, and exhausted, their spirit sapped by the horrors of war, thousands of families in the former socialist bloc are struggling to survive.

Unless they get help, the added burden of winter may prove too much for these families and many will not live to see the spring.

The Red Cross is already working hard to prevent that happening. We are the only agency to get through the front lines and deliver aid to where it's most needed. We are already shipping tents, water and sanitation kits to UN refugee camps. Where necessary, we charter helicopters to get supplies to villages in remote areas. But as winter drags on, we desperately need your help to send more supplies of Red Cross Winter Survival Packs to freezing and hungry families.

A Red Cross food parcel feeds a family for a month.

Red Cross Winter Survival Packs contain the best combination of food, blankets and plastic sheeting needed to get a refugee family through the winter.

A £15 gift from you would fill a Pack with enough supplies to feed a family of four for a month. £50 would buy a pack of blankets to keep a family of five warm throughout the winter. And £100 would provide enough plastic sheeting to keep the cold out of 10 temporary shelters.

As winter marches on, these families are in a race against time. Hundreds of innocent and vulnerable people are depending on Red Cross Winter Survival Packs. The sooner you help us, the sooner we can act, the better their chances of survival.

Emergency Red Cross supplies mean refugee children can be immunised against disease.

The Red Cross will not stand by and let winter sap away the strength of families who have already been through so much. Please send your gift today and help us deliver the Winter Survival Packs and give thousands of families a fighting chance to see another springtime in Eastern Europe.

Yours faithfully

Pierre Townsend
International Aid Department

21 Imagine your group is going to establish a new charity. What do you feel strongly about, as a local, national or international cause? Discuss and agree on a good cause.

   a   Choose a name for your charity. How can you make it memorable?
   b   Design a symbol or logo. How can you make it instantly recognisable?

22 Your charity is going to send an appeal letter to the general public. First study the Red Cross letter again, this time focusing on structure and style.

   a   List the different stages of the letter.
   b   How would you describe the adjectives (e.g. *sad, fierce, deadly, bitter*)?
   c   What is the effect of the use of lists?
   d   Why does it begin *Dear Supporter*?
   e   What effect do the subject pronouns *we, you* and *they* have?
   f   Where and why is repetition used?
   g   Why do you think the word *family* is mentioned so often?
   h   What can you say about paragraph length and sentence structure?
   i   Are the tone and style formal or informal, or both?

23 Look at the visual features and the layout of the Red Cross letter. Which parts stand out most? Why? List the layout and graphic devices used.

▼ *Exam tip!*

Layout is an aspect of the art of persuasion. A persuasive text for a mass audience is risking failure if it is unattractive or too densely arranged on the page. Whether you are producing coursework by hand or on a keyboard, the following devices can be used to break up text blocks and give variety and visual appeal: coloured type, capitals, captions, size changes, boxes, bold type, underlining, asterisks, bullets, headings, sub-headings, wide margins, blank lines. But remember: it is your English language skills which are being assessed, not your artistic or technological ability!

---

24 Divide responsibilities for different areas or aspects of your charity's appeal letter among the members of the group. Each person should research, plan and present ideas to the rest of the group for approval. The responsibilities could be divided as follows:

   • illustrations and captions
   • structure and layout design
   • factual and statistical research
   • selection and writing of content
   • proofreading and editing

You may already know about your chosen topic. If not, use the school library, the Internet, magazine articles or newspapers as resources for information and illustrations, bearing in mind that the downloading and reproducing of unaltered source material counts as plagiarism, and will be penalised.

25 Write the appeal letter, combining the contributions of each group member. Use the ideas from and answers to Exercises 18–24.

You may word-process your letter to make it look more authentic and accessible, or use different types and colours of handwriting and stick pictures on.

26 Develop your appeal letter into a script to be used on the radio or as a television voice-over for a charity appeal broadcast. The speech must be exactly three minutes long to fit the slot.

- Discuss as a group and select the material from each letter which would be most appropriate and effective for this purpose and audience.
- Consider reordering or rephrasing some of the material.
- Choose someone in your group to do the reading aloud, and help her/him to practise a persuasive delivery.
- Video- or audio-tape the broadcasts, and replay them to the class.

Class members should vote individually on which charity they feel persuaded to donate money to as a result of the broadcasts.

Further practice

a You would really like to go on holiday with some friends this year, instead of with your family as usual. List and order the facts and points you would use to persuade your parents to let you go, and anticipate their objections. Write a conversation of one and a half sides between you and a parent, in which you succeed in persuading her/him.

b You are going to start and run a club at your school. Write a handout to pass round and display on notice boards to persuade students to join. Tell them the club's name, what you propose it will do and why they should want to join. Write about one side.

c Study the set of facts about a donkey sanctuary on page 94. Order the information, add extra details and write a leaflet to promote the charity. You may need to look up some words in a dictionary. Try to use the material in an eye-catching way. Look at the exam tip after Exercise 23 to remind you of possible techniques.

Friends of the Cyprus Donkey

4772 Vouni Village

Member of the World Society for the Protection of Animals (WSPA)

Phone: 357 2594 5488 (Visitor Centre)

E-mail: donkeycy@cytanet.com.cy

Opening hours: Monday to Saturday, 10.00 a.m. to 4.00 p.m.

Admission – Adults and Children over 12: C£1; Members, Adopters and Children under 12: free

Annual Membership £12 sterling per year; Family Membership £20 sterling per year; Life Membership £80 sterling

Adopt a donkey for a year: cost £12 sterling, which provides 25 feeds. Choose a donkey and get a certificate with photograph.

Twice-yearly newsletter for all Members and Adopters

Sanctuary occupies a number of fields around the village of Vouni and has 12 enclosures.

Visitor Centre has shop, refreshments, donkey treats, hillside walk and picnic area.

Animals are taken out to graze in winter and spring, when there is fresh grass.

The association has a mobile clinic and employs a vet, dentist and farrier.

By prior arrangement, donkeys may be taken for walks by Members and Adopters in the nearby hills.

Friends of the Cyprus Donkey Sanctuary was founded in 1994.

It cares for old, sick and unwanted donkeys.

It provides medical and animal welfare services to owners of working donkeys throughout Cyprus.

Unit 11: *Composition*

This unit introduces and practises the skills of approaching personal and creative narrative writing.

> ▼ *Exam tip!*
>
> Narrative must have event and character, as together these make up the storyline. Narrative can be the most enjoyable type of writing to read, provided that the reader is engaged. You must not only tell an interesting story, but create a setting and an atmosphere for it. The reader needs a sense of time, place and weather to be able to picture the scene. Whether it is serious or amusing, sad or cheerful will depend on how you choose your vocabulary. Narrative is usually written in the past tense, the natural mode for telling about something which has already happened.

❶ Read the extract from an autobiography below. It is by Laurie Lee, a writer who left home in 1936 to fight in the Spanish Civil War.

As I Walked Out One Midsummer Morning

The stooping figure of my mother, waist-deep in the grass and caught there like a piece of sheep's wool, was the last I saw of my country home as I left it to discover the world. She stood old and bent at the top of the bank, silently watching me go, one gnarled red hand raised in farewell and blessing, not questioning why I went. At the bend of the road I looked back again and saw the gold light die behind her; then I turned the corner, passed the village school, and closed that part of my life for ever.

It was a bright Sunday morning in early June, the right time to be leaving home. I was nineteen years old, still soft at the edges, but with a confident belief in good fortune. I carried a small rolled-up tent, a violin in a blanket, a change of clothes and a tin of treacle biscuits. As I left home that morning and walked away from the sleeping village, it never occurred to me that others had done this before me.

And now I was on my journey, in a pair of thick boots and with a hazel stick in my hand. Naturally, I was going to London, which lay a hundred miles to the east; and it seemed equally obvious that I should go on foot. But first, as I'd never yet seen the sea, I thought I'd walk to the coast and find it. I had all the summer and all time to spend.

❷ Explain why this passage does or does not engage your interest as a reader.

With your partner, identify the imagery, details and adjectives which have been used to create

a character   b setting   c atmosphere

Explain why, in each case, the words/phrases are effective.

Exam tip! See next page ▶

Although a composition may be mainly narrative in intention, you can make it original and interesting by including other elements:
- reflections (thoughts and attitudes)
- emotions (feelings and memories)
- descriptions (of people and places)

❸ Read the diary entry below, written by a girl called Zlata in Sarajevo, in the former Yugoslavia, now in Bosnia-Herzogovina, in 1992. She calls her diary 'Mimmy'.

Dear Mimmy,

Today was truly, absolutely the worst day ever in Sarajevo. The shooting started around noon. Mummy and I moved into the hall. Daddy was in his office, under our flat, at the time. We told him on the interphone to run quickly to the downstairs lobby where we'd meet him. We brought Cicko [Zlata's canary] with us. The gunfire was getting worse, and we couldn't get over the wall to the Bobars, so we ran down to our own cellar.

The cellar is ugly, dark, smelly. Mummy, who's terrified of mice, had two fears to cope with. The three of us were in the same corner as the other day. We listened to the pounding shells, the shooting, the thundering noise overhead. We even heard planes. At one moment I realised that this awful cellar was the only place that could save our lives. Suddenly, it started to look almost warm and nice. It was the only way we could defend ourselves against all this terrible shooting. We heard glass shattering in our street. Horrible. I put my fingers in my ears to block out the terrible sounds. I was worried about Cicko. We had left him behind in the lobby. Would he catch cold there? Would something hit him? I was terribly hungry and thirsty. We had left our half-cooked lunch in the kitchen.

When the shooting died down a bit, Daddy ran over to our flat and brought us back some sandwiches. He said he could smell something burning and that the phones weren't working. He brought our TV set down to the cellar. That's when we learned that the main post office (near us) was on fire and that they had kidnapped our president. At around 20.00 we went back up to our flat. Almost every window in our street was broken. The place is knee-deep in glass. We're worried about Grandma and Grandad. Tomorrow, if we can go out, we'll see how they are. A terrible day. This has been the worst, most awful day in my eleven-year-old life. I hope it will be the only bad one.

Mummy and Daddy are very edgy. I have to go to bed.

Ciao

Source: Adapted from *Zlata's Diary: a child's life in Sarajevo*, Viking, 1994

❹ Without looking back at the passage yet, tell your teacher what has stayed in your mind from reading this narrative about a town and family under bombardment. How has the atmosphere of fear and destruction been made shocking or memorable?

5 What can you tell about the three characters mentioned in the diary entry: Zlata, her mother and her father? Write a sentence for each which says something about her/his personality.

6 With your partner, discuss which of the facts below are essential for a reader to be told about the main character of a narrative. Tick your choices. Compare your decisions with the rest of the class, and give your reasoning. Is there any other information you would wish to know?

name	age	marital status
occupation	eye colour	hair colour
facial appearance	nationality	current abode
education	body shape	clothing style
hobbies	family members	qualifications

7 How can you tell that the diary entry was written by a child? With your partner, list as much evidence as you can.

> **▼ Exam tip!**
>
> The extract consists of simple syntax and vocabulary. Sometimes in compositions a short sentence – or even a non-sentence – can be dramatically effective, especially at the beginning or end, or at a climactic moment. Remember, however, that complex sentences are generally the best way of expressing yourself with variety and economy, and of proving your command of English grammar. Avoid beginning every sentence with its subject, or using *then*, which is monotonous and unnecessary in chronological writing. In an IGCSE Composition task you need to show the range of your vocabulary: try not to repeat words, and use ambitious vocabulary whenever possible.

8 Write a short piece of first-person, autobiographical narrative called either *A frightening experience* or *An embarrassing moment*.

Write about three paragraphs, as in the passages in Exercises 1 and 3. Think first about situation, then about your characters and setting, and finally about your style, use of detail, and choice of vocabulary. Bear in mind the advice given in the unit so far.

When you have planned and written your piece – which could be the beginning of an exam practice or coursework composition – read it to the class.

> **▼ Exam tip!**
>
> Using your personal experience as the basis for continuous writing coursework or exam composition will help your writing to be original and authentic, and make it easier for you to think of something to write about. You can also use incidents which happened to someone else, either in reality or in a book or film. You are free to narrate in the first person (*I*) or third person (*he* or *she*), but remember that a first-person narrator cannot die at the end! Because the aim of narrative is to amuse or entertain, not to inform or to stick to the truth, you can exaggerate, adapt, add or remove things, and do whatever will make your story more engaging. Don't try to cover too much time or too many incidents; one or two main events and two or three characters are usually enough.

9 Read the following extract from Susan Hill's ghost story *The Woman in Black*. (Spider is a dog.)

After a while, I heard the odd sound again. It seemed to be coming from along the passage to my left, at the far end. But it was still quite impossible to identify. Very cautiously, listening, hardly breathing, I ventured a few steps in that direction. Spider went ahead of me. The passage led only to three other bedrooms on either side and, one by one, regaining my nerve as I went, I opened them and looked inside each one. Nothing, only heavy old furniture and empty unmade beds and, in the rooms at the back of the house, moonlight. Down below me on the ground floor of the house, silence, a seething, blanketing, almost tangible silence, and a musty darkness, thick as felt.

And then I reached the door at the very end of the passage. Spider was there before me and her body, as she sniffed beneath it, went rigid, her growling grew louder. I put my hand on her collar, stroked the rough, short hair, as much for my own reassurance as for hers. I could feel the tension in her limbs and body and it answered to my own.

This was the door without a keyhole, which I had been unable to open on my first visit to Eel Marsh House. I had no idea what was beyond it. Except the sound.

10 Suspense is an important feature of narrative writing. With your partner, underline the words/phrases that create an atmosphere of fear and expectancy in this extract.

11 Now read the extract below from a short story by Alan Paton called *The Wasteland*, in which an elderly man is trying to escape from a gang of youths who intend to steal his money.

So trapped was he that he was filled suddenly with strength and anger, and he ran towards the waste land swinging his heavy stick. In the darkness a form loomed up at him, and he swung at it, and heard it give a cry of pain. Then he plunged blindly into the wilderness of wire and iron and the bodies of old cars.

Something caught him by the leg, and he brought his stick crashing down on it, but it was no man, only some knife-edged piece of iron. He was sobbing and out of breath but he pushed on into the waste, while behind him they pushed on also, knocking against the old iron bodies and kicking against tins and buckets. He fell into some grotesque shape of wire; it was barbed and tore at his clothes and flesh. Then it held him, so that it seemed to him that death must be near, and having no other hope, he cried out, 'Help, help me!' in what should have been a great voice, but was voiceless and gasping. He tore at the wire, and it tore at him too, ripping his face and his hands.

12 a Select from the above extract all the words/ short phrases which convey a feeling of danger or pain.

b Write comments to explain how the use of words and phrases achieves particular effects.

13 Discuss with your partner what features the two previous extracts have in common, or how they differ. Consider the following:

- sense of character
- danger of situation
- setting
- time of day
- references to noise or silence

- use of paragraphing
- use of adjectives and adverbs
- choice of verbs
- sentence structure
- pace (speed of events)

▼ *Exam tip!*   *relates to Exercises 9, 11 and 13*

Narrative writing can create tension with sinister adjectives and adverbs, and horror can be evoked by the use of violent verbs, especially those which give objects a human power. Suspense can be created by slowing the pace, so that there is a sense of waiting and nothing actually happens for a while (see Exercise 9), whereas panic is created by the opposite technique of using a lot of quick actions in a short time to suggest uncontrolled speed (as in Exercise 11). Paragraph breaks, sentence length and punctuation all affect the rhythm and tension of a piece of writing. Also notice that in both passages there is an unknown *it*; something mysterious arouses curiosity and this is often more frightening than a known and visible enemy. Many stories are spoiled by unconvincing gory description, and some of the best narratives are understated or leave something unexplained for the reader to think about.

---

14 Read aloud the poem below by the American poet Robert Frost, one line each around the class.

Stopping by Woods on a Snowy Evening

Whose woods these are I think I know.
His house is in the village, though;
He will not see me stopping here
To watch his woods fill up with snow.

My little horse must think it queer
To stop without a farmhouse near
Between the woods and frozen lake
The darkest evening of the year.

He gives his harness bells a shake
To ask if there is some mistake.
The only other sound's the sweep
Of easy wind and downy flake.

The woods are lovely, dark, and deep,
But I have promises to keep,
And miles to go before I sleep,
And miles to go before I sleep.

15 The poem describes the setting, but the situation and characters have been left mysterious. Think of a basic storyline which would fit the poem, and write the first sentence of your story. Share it with the rest of the class, and vote for the opening which would most make the reader want to read on.

16 Most narrative openings fall into one of six categories:

1 middle of the action
2 setting the scene/atmosphere
3 introducing the main character
4 middle of the dialogue
5 shock (unexpected)
6 intrigue (mystery)

Which type did you use in Exercise 15?

17 In small groups, study the opening sentences to published narratives below:

a Say which of the six types they are, using the numbers in Exercise 16. (Some openings are combinations of the basic types.)
b Give each opening a mark out of 10, based on your desire to continue reading.
c Report your conclusions on the best openings to the rest of the class, giving reasons.

A It was a bright cold day in April, and the clocks were striking thirteen.
B Robert Cohn was once middleweight boxing champion of Princeton.
C It was the coldest winter in the Alps in living memory.
D As Gregor Samsa awoke one morning from uneasy dreams he found himself transformed in his bed into a gigantic insect.
E True! – nervous – very, very dreadfully nervous I had been and am!
F 'Not that horse, mister.'
G So, the dreadful old woman was dead at last.
H There was nothing special about number Forty-Seven.
I Lonely and boring the hours stretched endlessly ahead.
J When Floyd Anselmo saw the purple cow grazing on a hillside of his dairy range one cold morning in October he thought his mind must be hallucinating.
K He was never called Ekky now, because he was getting to be a real boy, nearly six, with grey flannel trousers that had a separate belt and weren't kept up by elastic, and his name was Eric.
L Andrea looked out of the curtains as soon as she woke.
M Last night I dreamed I was at Manderley again.
N Hale knew they meant to murder him before he had been in Brighton three hours.
O An arbitrary choice then, a definitive moment: October 23, 1990.
P 'Attention,' a voice began to call, and it was as though an oboe had suddenly become articulate.
Q Only the steady creaking of a flight of swans disturbed the silence, labouring low overhead with outstretched necks towards the sea.
R When Bill Simpson woke up on Monday morning, he found he was a girl.

S 'Lizzy!' she exclaimed, flinging open the door. 'Are you okay?'

T Peter was crammed onto a narrow ledge which sloped down towards a terrible abyss.

U It wasn't a human.

V A moment's silence, and then a whistle blew and the garden became filled with moving shadows and running footsteps.

W The Iron Man came to the top of the cliff.

X Fugu is a fish caught off the Pacific shores of Japan.

Y 'How did that alligator get in the bath?' demanded my father one morning at breakfast.

Z The house shook, the windows rattled, a framed photograph slipped off the shelf and fell into the hearth.

18 Write one of each of the six types of opening sentence listed in Exercise 16, using the title *My first day at school*. Show your sentences to your partner, who will choose the one s/he likes best.

19 Now write the final sentence for your story. How would you describe the type of ending you have used?

▼ *Exam tip!*

Endings should reward the reader for having read your story. An anti-climactic, predictable or overused ending (such as *and then I woke up*) will disappoint the reader and weaken your composition. A satisfying ending can be

- a 'cliffhanger' (e.g. *But just at that moment, the phone rang.*)
- a short piece of humorous, dramatic or ironic direct speech (e.g. *There's something I didn't tell you: the cat can talk!*)
- an unexpected twist (e.g. *The Wasteland* ends with the man discovering that his attacker, whom he has killed in self-defence, was his own son)
- a return to the beginning (e.g. repeating the first sentence or referring to the event which began the story)
- 'happily-ever-after' (e.g. *Shortly afterwards, they agreed to get married.*)
- an open ending (e.g. *No one knows if they ever learned the truth.*)
- a sense of finality (e.g. *And that was the last time I ever saw my best friend.*)

Choose an ending which fits the mood of the story and provides a conclusion. You don't want to sound as if you simply ran out of time, space or ideas. You should know your ending before you start so that you can work towards it, without spoiling the suspense by giving it away.

---

20 Dialogue can be used within a narrative, as well as at the beginning or end. Discuss the following questions with your partner:

a What does direct speech contribute to a story?

b At what points in a narrative is dialogue likely to be effective?

21 Think of an event which could be expressed as dialogue in your composition *My first day at school*. Write the dialogue.

Exam tip! See next page ▶

22 Did you use the verb *said* in the last exercise? With your partner, list all the more precise and interesting verbs you can think of for reporting speech. Examples have been provided.

shouted   *muttered*

▼ *Exam tip!* relates to Exercises 21 and 22

Dialogue is most effective in narrative at points of **tension**, drama and **climax**. It is pointless for everyday comments (e.g. *'Goodbye,' she said. 'Goodbye,' he said.*), as it simply holds up the story without contributing anything to it (and annoys the reader!). It also ceases to be effective if you use it too often and your writing becomes a script rather than a composition. Appropriately used, however, speech can help to convey characters' personalities and relationships, especially if the characters speak in a different style from each other.

23 Discuss with your partner possible storylines behind the pictures below. Agree on a convincing dialogue for the situation in each of the pictures. Do not use the verb *said,* and try to make the two characters talk in different ways to differentiate their personalities. Give them three short speeches each.

A    B

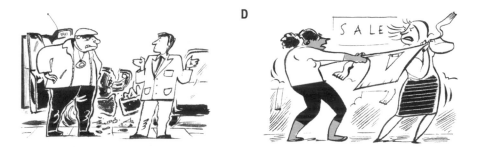

24 Write one of the dialogues in Exercise 22, taking care with the layout and punctuation. When you have finished, swap with your partner and mark each other's work, circling each mistake. Give it back for correction.

▼ *Exam tip!*

Remember the rules for setting out dialogue in a narrative:
- Start a new line or paragraph for a change of speaker.
- Use double inverted commas at the beginning and end of the speech.
- Use a full stop, comma, question mark or exclamation mark at the end of every speech (and inside the final inverted commas).
- Use a capital letter to begin a speech, even in the middle of a sentence.
- Use the same punctuation within a speech as you would for ordinary sentences.

25 With your partner, perform your dialogue to the class. They must try to guess which picture it relates to, and comment on how effective it would be as dialogue within a narrative.

26 Share with the class a lateral-thinking puzzle you know of. These take the form of mini-narratives which could be used as inspiration for a narrative composition with a mystery or 'twist in the tale'. Here is an example:

Gemma and Glen have been found dead, lying on a wet floor and covered in broken glass, but with no injuries. What happened? (Answer: Gemma and Glen are goldfish. The cat knocked their bowl off the table.)

27 Below are eight narrative composition titles with which to practise your planning skills. Make sure that each plan pays attention to opening and ending, and contains at least seven topic headings (and would become about 400 words). Indicate where dialogue and description would be included, the time frame of the narrative and where the story's climax will occur.

    a *'I had to think quickly if I was to stay out of trouble.' Continue this opening sentence to a story.*
    b *The box*
    c *No regrets*
    d *An incredible journey*
    e *The letter which arrived too late*
    f *Write a story which involves a cat, a shop, a ticket and a robbery.*
    g *Look before you leap.*
    h *'A thing of beauty is a joy for ever.' Write a story inspired by this line of poetry.*

> **▼ Exam tip!**
>
> Narrative titles can take different forms: short phrase, quotation, proverb, continuation of opening sentence. You may not be required to write a complete story. Bear in mind the many kinds of narrative – such as science fiction, supernatural, comedy, detective. There is no reason why you should not write an exam composition or coursework piece in any of these genres. Don't attempt to reproduce a piece of writing you have done before, however, as it is likely to sound dull and may not be fully relevant to the exam title.

28 Compare plans with your partner. Your plans for the same title will probably be very different. Advise each other on which ones would most likely turn into a good narrative composition.

29 Choose one of your plans from Exercise 27 to turn into a mini-saga, which is a complete narrative consisting of exactly 50 words. You will need to draft and edit until you get it exactly right, considering which content is essential and how the use of grammar and sentence structure affects the word count. Read your mini-saga to the rest of the class, which will vote on a winner.

Further practice

a   Complete the composition you started in Exercise 8.

b   Choose five opening sentences from Exercise 17 and write first-paragraph continuations for them.

c   Choose your best plan from Exercise 27 and develop it into a narrative composition.

> ▼ *Exam tip!*
>
> Check your compositions, and continue to improve them, after you have finished. To achieve a high mark in an IGCSE composition task you must have stylistic maturity, demonstrate structure, show a clear sense of audience, and make few or no mistakes. To achieve a top grade for 'Style and accuracy' you must also use 'a variety of well-made sentences, including sophisticated complex sentences'.

Part 3 People: society, lifestyles, relationships

Unit 12: *Speaking and listening*

This unit offers opportunities for the group-discussion activities required for Speaking and Listening coursework, and practises expressing opinions.

▼ *Exam tip!*

In Speaking and listening tasks a 'discussion' is not a casual conversation on a trivial topic, in which interruptions and colloquialisms are acceptable, but a more formal and serious interaction based on an exchange of ideas which extends the subject matter using informative detail to support opinions.

1 Why do you think people take part in discussions? With your partner, list examples of small-group discussion situations and their purposes in a grid like the one below. An example has been provided.

Situation	Purpose
state visits between presidents	to improve relations and trade

Can it be right that 400 boxing fans are paying £6 each to watch a schoolgirl fight?

MOST of her classmates *idolise* David Beckham or Robbie Williams.

But 14-year-old Joanne Kiely worships the boxer Naseem Hamed.

And next month she hopes to emulate him when she fights a girl of 15 in front of hundreds of paying, baying spectators.

The bout between Joanne and Jain McQuire was condemned by the medical profession yesterday.

But it was defended by boxing's governing body, which only last week received nearly £13 million from National Lottery funds.

The schoolgirls will make their debut in the ring at a boxing evening at Stockport Town Hall on May 10. Some 400 fight fans are expected to pay £6 each to attend.

The youngsters, who both weigh 9st 2lb, have trained for the three 90-second rounds for months. They will wear headguards, abdominal protectors and breastplates.

Aping the tough-talking style of her idol Hamed, Joanne – from Offerton, Greater Manchester – *boasted* that she hoped to knock out her Liverpudlian opponent in the first round. 'I've been building up to this for months,' she added.

'It was a bit frustrating because there weren't any girls to take on. But then the organisers managed to find an *opponent* on the Internet. I'm really looking forward to it.'

Joanne, who attends Offerton High School, is *coached* by her 36-year-old father Tony. Mr Kiely is an ex-boxer, like his father before him.

Her mother Mary accused those who criticise all-girl boxing of *hypocrisy*, claiming: '*Martial* arts are much more dangerous. Some of them have children as young as five competing.'

Joanne also defended her decision to box. 'Some local mums have said I should take dancing classes instead but that doesn't bother me,' she said. 'Boxing teaches you self-defence, builds your confidence and keeps you fit.'

Female boxing was illegal in Britain as recently as four years ago but the *restrictions* crumbled in the face of sex *discrimination* laws.

In 1998, welterweight Jane Couch, from Fleetwood, Lancashire, overturned the ban on professional fights when she won a sex discrimination claim after being refused a licence to box.

In the same year, Emma Brammer, 14, won a bout on points in front of hundreds of cheering fans at a Leicester working men's club after giving her opponent, 13-year-old Andrea Prime, a bloody nose.

Seven women boxers are currently licensed by the British Boxing Board of Control, its spokesman said yesterday.

The Amateur Boxing Association recognises fights between girls over 11 who pass a medical.

Up to 15 bouts involving girls under 16 have taken place since last September.

Many more girls are in training. But fights are difficult to organise because of the different rates at which girls mature. An age gap of one year between opponents – or 4lb 6 oz in weight – is the maximum permitted.

The British Medical Association, which wants a ban on all boxing, condemned licensed fights between women as 'a demented extension of equal opportunities'.

A spokesman said: 'Boxing's *apologists* say it's a good way for children to get rid of *excess* energy and *aggression*. But plenty of other sports do that without putting them in danger of damaging their brains and their eyes.'

The spokesman went on to criticise Sport England's decision to grant the Amateur Boxing Association £12.75 million of *Lottery* money, particularly as there was nothing to prevent the cash being used to support children's boxing.

The Stockport fight's promoter, Peter McDonald, defended it, saying: 'There's nothing wrong with girls boxing in this day and age of sexual equality.'

He cautioned, however: 'It's their first bout so I wouldn't expect too much. They're only children.'

Source: *Daily Mail,* 19 April 2001

2 Read the newspaper article on girls' boxing opposite as preparation for a group discussion.

3 Ten words are underlined in the article. With your partner, match the words to their definitions, then check them in a dictionary.

emulate	person who arranges sporting events
baying	at this moment
bout	try to be like (someone because you admire her/him)
debut	as if crazy
aping	first public appearance
frustrating	copying (someone's behaviour)
crumbled	shouts and demands made by a crowd at a contest
currently	causing impatience, discouraging
demented	boxing or wrestling match
promoter	broke up and lost all power

4 Do you know or can you guess the meanings of the following 12 words italicised in the article? Work with your partner to find synonyms or give definitions.

a	idolise	e	hypocrisy	i	apologists
b	boasted	f	Martial	j	excess
c	opponent	g	restrictions	k	aggression
d	coached	h	discrimination	l	Lottery

Check your answers in a dictionary. Add the words you did not know to your personal vocabulary list.

5 Some of the statements in the article are facts; others are opinions. With your partner, find five examples of each and put them into two columns in note form. Examples have been provided.

Fact	Opinion
Joanne is 14	Joanne expects to win in first round

6 Scan the article for verbs. Using two different colours, highlight fact verbs and opinion verbs. What do you notice?

▼ Exam tip!

One skill you need to develop as a response to written and spoken texts, and when planning talks, is the ability to distinguish between fact and opinion. Journalism mixes the two; and the lower its quality, the more it uses opinion rather than fact. Certain verbs help you to identify which is which:

- Facts tend to be introduced by *is, does, can, will, has, proves, shows*.
- Opinions tend to be introduced by *hopes, claims, thinks, believes, expects, accuses, suggests*.

7 Discuss as a class your response to the boxing article. Here are some ideas to help you:

   a Do you find anything about it surprising or offensive?

   b Judging from the headline, what do you think the reporter thinks about this issue?

   c What is your own attitude to boxing as a sport generally?

   d Which side are you on as regards girls boxing, and why?

   e Do the boys and girls in your class hold different views? If so, why?

▼ *Exam tip!*

When taking part in group discussion, don't dominate it by talking too much, nor say so little that your views are not expressed. You must not interrupt other speakers. Listen attentively to their views so that you can respond to them. The aim is to follow on from what the previous speaker has said by agreeing or disagreeing, and by adding a new fact or opinion to the discussion. Evidence to support your point of view will give it greater impact. You might cite statistics, events reported in the media, or your own experience or that of someone you know.

---

8 Read the extract below, which is from an interview between an American news agency reporter and Jamie Bell, the actor who played the ballet dancer Billy Elliot in the film of that name.

CNN	You share similarities with Billy Elliot, but one big difference is the age at which you developed an interest in ballet. How long have you been dancing?
Bell	Since I was 6.
CNN	You are now 14 years old; how did you hide ballet from your friends for so long?
Bell	Well, I just didn't tell them, … and when they used to say, 'Are you coming out to play tonight?' I'd say, 'No, I am going to the doctor's,' or 'I have to visit my nana in the hospital,' or something. So they didn't know where I was going.
CNN	How did your friends react when they found out?
Bell	Well, most of my closest friends were fine, but it was mostly the kids that I didn't really know that … said 'girlie boy' or 'ballerina boy'. But most of that gave me more determination to do it, because I wanted to prove to them that [ballet] wasn't just for girls; it was for boys as well.

Source: Adapted from http://www.cnn.com

9 With your partner, discuss the following:

   a your response to what Jamie Bell says above

   b your views on or experience of ballet

   c how your response to Jamie the ballet dancer compares with your response to Joanne the boxer

10 With your partner, look at the statements below:

Joanne says: *Some local mums have said I should take dancing classes instead but that doesn't bother me.*

Jamie says: *I wanted to prove to them that [ballet] wasn't just for girls.*

a In one sentence, summarise the issue under discussion in both extracts.
b In one sentence, describe what the two characters have in common as personalities.
c In one sentence, say why you think this issue arouses such strong feelings.

Compare your answers to those of the rest of the class.

11 In groups of four or more students, hold a discussion on the subject of gender-divided sports and professions. Your teacher will circulate, listen to, assess and give feedback on your performance in your group.

You may wish to comment on

- school PE lessons
- military service
- international athletics
- traditionally male jobs (e.g. soldier, engineer)
- traditionally female jobs (e.g. nurse, primary school teacher)

12 Read the newspaper report on page 110 as preparation for a discussion. The article is about a fan of Paul McCartney, a musician and former member of the famous British pop group The Beatles.

13 In groups of four or five, hold a discussion which takes the report as a starting point. Express your views about the behaviour of Evenko, and then move on to the idea of fanaticism generally:

- What are the characteristics of a fan?
- What kinds of pursuits attract fans?
- What makes someone become a fanatic?
- What are the attractions/benefits of being a fan?
- What are the dangers of fanaticism?

As you speak and listen, think about which comments being made in the discussion are facts and which are opinions. Try to have a balance between the two. Also try to adopt an appropriate level of formality.

Exam tip! See next page ▶

During the discussion, you will be expected to give a point of view and to support it. This is a sophisticated speaking skill, requiring you not only to consider content but also expression and tone of voice, so that you make your opinions clear without sounding aggressive or disrespectful. Avoid extreme adverbs – such as *obviously, totally, utterly* – as they will make you sound dogmatic and unwilling to consider views different from your own. You are required for assessment purposes to 'Listen to and respond appropriately to the contributions of others' (S5) and to treat other members of the group as equals.

From Russia with luck

Hers is an extraordinary story. Until three weeks ago 20-year-old Evenko, a student from the Urals, had never left Russia, yet she made a 3,000 mile journey to the small Welsh border town of Hay-on-Wye, where McCartney was reading from *Blackbird Singing*, the poetry collection he published earlier this year.

'My mother thinks I am visiting friends near Moscow. I said I would be away for 20 days. When she finds out where I am, she's going to kill me,' admitted Evenko.

A Beatles fan since the age of 10, she started making plans to visit Britain in the spring. 'I'm doing strawberry-picking on a farm near Taunton, Somerset. When I discovered that Paul was in Britain reading his poetry, I had to be here. For me, the Beatles are more important than eating or drinking.'

With a sleeping bag and a back-pack, Evenko started hitch-hiking from her home city of Cheliabinsk to Taunton after she had been tipped off about the event in an e-mail from another Beatles fan.

But she had no idea where in Britain the reading was taking place. And she had no ticket.

Evenko left Taunton's strawberry fields on the last leg of her epic journey. Seven lifts later, she joined the fans lining the streets of the town and brandished her placard appealing for a ticket. A man whose friend was ill sold her his spare ticket for its cover price.

McCartney's entourage were so touched by her story that they are sending her a signed copy of his poems, and festival organisers arranged accommodation and a square meal for her, then a rather more luxurious return journey to Taunton in one of the festival's limousines.

'I have no words to explain my feelings. You know, when your dreams come true?' Evenko says. Now she has one ambition: to invite McCartney to play in her home city. 'The Beatles never came to Russia. Maybe after this day he might visit.'

Source: Adapted from *The Sunday Times*, 3 June 2001

14 Rewrite the following informal speech in a formal way, then read it to the class:

This is the six o'clock news. Now, let me see, oh yeah … there's been a fantastic traffic jam in central Paris this afternoon, you know – really amazing – went on for, oh I dunno, about three hours, more or less, before the police turned up and, like, sorted it. Oh, and another thing, the poor old Prime Minister got stuck in it too…

▼ Exam tip!

Part of the skill of speaking well is to know when formal language is required and when it is acceptable to be informal. In classroom discussion – even though it is between peers/ friends – use a formal mode of expression which is appropriate to the task, shows respect for others, and which demonstrates your ability to 'Use language and register appropriate to audience and context' (S4).

---

15 In groups of three or four, study the photograph below. What thoughts and feelings does it evoke? Hold a discussion about the situation and its implications. Your teacher will listen to part of each group's discussion.

Teenage horoscopes

Aries

 A powerful aspect to Mars in your sign makes you majorly passionate. You feel very strongly today and may come across as more aggressive than you really are. Careful now – you don't want to frighten anyone. (If you DO, on the other hand, then you might as well go for it. You're well scary.)

Taurus

 Because the Moon forms a dodgy aspect to your ruling planet Saturn today, you could be feeling a bit negative (to say the least). Stop going on about all the stuff you don't like and don't want, and stop taking yourself so seriously. Angels can fly because they know how to lighten up – there's a thought for you...

Gemini

 A couple of tense aspects to the Moon in your sign means the last thing you want to do is stay in and tidy your room today. If this is what's expected of you, you could have a fight on your hands. You need to be free to do what you want (within reason of course) today, and if anyone tries to clip those flapping wings of yours, they could be in for a shock.

Cancer

 Today's Moon/Neptune conjunction makes you almost hyper-aware of other people's needs and feelings. Because you're extra sensitive today, there's no doubt that their moods can seriously affect yours. That's why it'd be a good idea to keep away from grumpy folk today. Stay with the happy, smiley folk (well, until they start to get on your nerves anyway...).

Leo

 Today's depressing aspect to Saturn in Taurus affects you in that today everything seems so much worse than it actually is. Wallowing around in misery is only going to make matters worse. So make an effort to look at all the good things and to realise just how lucky you actually are. (Loads of your mates would give anything to be in your shoes – and that's not just because you have nice shoes...)

Virgo

 A dodgy aspect between the Moon and your ruler Mercury means your emotions get the better of you today when trying to get a message across to someone. For some reason, this person reacts as if you're speaking a different language, which totally enrages you. You're usually so cool, so try not to go ballistic: it won't do your image any good.

Libra

 Today's tricky aspect between your ruling planet Mercury and the Moon means that your emotions seem to get the better of you, and you end up not being able to make a firm decision about anything. Sit tight for now and leave the decisions for another day.

Scorpio

 A powerful aspect between the Moon and your ruling planet Mars makes it difficult for you to see anything in an objective way. If you need to make a choice today, it could be tricky, as you can only see things in relation to yourself right now. Wait till this transit has passed (it'll be over by tomorrow) and you'll be able to think more clearly and come to sensible conclusions more quickly.

Sagittarius

 The conjunction of the Moon and Mercury in your opposite sign means you're more emotional than usual today when it comes to very close relationships. Although this is well received by loved ones, today is not the best day to make an important decision. It's a good time to work out how you REALLY feel: once you're sure about that, then – and only then – will you be able to make a sensible choice.

Capricorn

 The sensitive aspect between the emotional Moon and your ruling planet Pluto means that today you're likely to feel everything very intensely. Money matters and all the stuff going on at home are occupying you right now. Don't even try to focus on anything else today – you won't be able to. Just sort out these problems once and for all or you'll be distracted indefinitely. And that won't do.

Aquarius

 A tricky Moon/Mercury aspect in the social part of your chart means you could have trouble getting a friend to see things your way. You're usually so together, but today your emotions get the better of you, and you end up a jibbering heap. This could mean that this evening's plans will be changed in some way. But don't feel bad about it. A change is as good as a rest (so 'they' say), so enjoy having a totally different Wednesday night.

Pisces

A strong aspect between passionate Mars and your ruler the Moon makes you feel extremely powerful today. Your feelings may be running a little high though and because your views may be a bit extreme right now, you'd do well to keep a few of them to yourself – especially if nobody has actually asked you for them. Consider yourself told.

16 Look at the horoscopes from a teenage magazine opposite. Assess the level of formality of the style, giving examples.

17 How do you feel about astrology? Is it a science? Do you usually read your horoscope in magazines? Why or why not? Why do some people depend on them?

Take five minutes to prepare some ideas you could use in a class discussion on this topic, using the text opposite for quotations and examples.

When the discussion takes place, make a contribution which follows on from that of the previous speaker and which expresses and supports a viewpoint.

Further practice

a What type of school or college do you attend? Why do you go to this type of school? Do you intend to go to university? Prepare brief notes for a discussion on secondary, further or higher education which adopt and support a view.

b Who or what are you a fan of? Prepare headings for a contribution to a discussion on your favourite topic.

c Below is an example of urban graffiti in Brasilia. Do you think it is attractive and serves a useful purpose, or is it ugly and criminal? Write points, in two columns, for both sides of a discussion on the topic of graffiti.

Part 4 Ideas: art, science, technology

Unit 13: Reading

This unit continues to develop summary skills, the collation of implicit meanings and attitudes, and recognition of language effects. We also practise vocabulary building and advanced punctuation.

1 Read the article on the opposite page from a Sunday newspaper magazine.

2 Summarise each of the five paragraphs in the article in a short phrase or simple sentence. Compare with your partner and argue why yours are better.

3 Highlight the facts and the opinions in this article in different colours. Which are there more of? Is this what you expect in a text about science?

4 Complete the following summary statements, after scanning the text. Remember to reduce the number of words, and to change them into your own.

   a *Dean Radin's experiments suggest that some people...*
   b *His evidence is that...*
   c *Richard Wiseman suspects that people...*
   d *The existence of a sixth sense would be important in that...*
   e *The future of the planet could be affected because...*

5 Summarise what you have learned from this passage about the 'sixth sense' and the evidence for its existence. Write about half a side.

6 Read the magazine article on page 116, which describes how a Russian built and sailed his own submarine.

THE SIXTH SENSE

Ever been just about to call someone when the phone rings and the person in question is on the other end? Or have you experienced a sudden feeling of unease or danger, even though you're in a perfectly harmless situation? If you're a sceptic, you'll put it down to coincidence and an overactive imagination. But some people believe it is evidence that there is a sixth sense beyond smell, taste, touch, hearing and sight. Now, scientists are carrying out experiments to prove not only that it exists, but also to find out how you can use it to your advantage.

Dean Radin, a researcher in California, has set up the Boundary Institute in Los Altos and is currently using its website to recruit 4,000 people in 57 countries to find out if there are any true instances of sixth sense or, as he calls it, 'precognition' – the ability to predict outcomes. The results so far are extraordinary. In a card test, where you have to guess which of the five cards on a computer screen will be turned over to reveal a picture, the top scorers hit the right card 48% of the time – the odds against this happening are 2,669 to 1.

Meanwhile, Radin's most famous study involves subjects looking at a variety of images that are designed to provoke a specific response. The results show that some people start to respond in the appropriate way several seconds before the image is revealed. In the experiment, subjects sit alone in a room in front of a computer, with electrodes attached to their bodies to measure changes in skin resistance and blood flow, which are measures of arousal. The computer randomly selects an image that either provokes emotion (e.g. a road accident) or calms (e.g. trees). Radin has found that one in six people has a consistent rise in arousal before they see the road-accident-type pictures, while remaining calm before the tree-type pictures.

Not surprisingly, the scientific establishment remains sceptical about the whole area. 'While these experiments do show interesting results, you can't rule out the influence of what we call "sensory cueing" on the results – that the subjects are subliminally picking up the answers from the researchers. It's also impossible to do these experiments with a proper control group,' says Dr Richard Wiseman, a psychologist at the University of Hertfordshire.

But even if you do accept that a sixth sense exists, the question is, does it actually serve any purpose? Radin says it does. 'The future of our civilisation depends on decisions that are being made now, whether it's about how we farm our food, how we get rid of our waste or whether we allow chemicals to be included in everyday products. We don't have answers to these important questions, yet the decisions will affect our lives for decades or longer. Anything we can do to improve our ability to predict future events is well worth the effort', he says. 'If it turns out that some people can genuinely forecast the future some of the time, as I believe the data shows, then understanding this capability is as important as cutting-edge science.'

Source: Adapted from *The Sunday Times*, 22 April 2001

7 Would the following make good alternative headlines to the article on page 116? For each, say why or why not. Would any of them be better than the existing one? Can you think of an even better one? What does the rest of the class think?

a **Mikhail's mad invention**
b **Do-it-yourself submarine**
c **Pedal power**
d **KGB arrest spy suspect**
e **Seasick sailor's secret**

One man and his sub

Even in the often <u>surreal</u> world of inventions, Mikhail Puchkov's creation has to rank as one of the more <u>bizarre</u>: a pedal-powered one-man mini submarine.

Actually, he no longer needs the pedals, although they are still there at the front of his steel craft. 'I used to pedal for electricity, but that was too exhausting,' he says. So some time ago Puchkov installed a car battery and lengthened the craft to its present five metres. This scarcely qualifies as a <u>conventional</u> vessel. Surrounded by the masts of St Petersburg's Nautical Institute Yacht Club, where Puchkov is based in summer, the do-it-yourself submarine looks particularly out of place.

Sipping tea and smoking cigarettes in front of the club's rusty metal huts, Puchkov explains the basics of his invention. When he is on the surface he relies on an ordinary, if noisy, petrol-powered motorbike engine – starting it up sounds like someone drilling through a wall – and navigates by global positioning satellites. Underwater, he switches to an electric motor (now powered by the battery) and old-fashioned compasses and maps for navigation (there is no periscope). Oxygen is supplied from a bottle 'filled with normal air'. The sub goes to a maximum depth of 10 m and reaches a top speed of 8 km an hour, which, he observes, is '3 km per hour faster than the average person walks'.

This eccentric device, shaped rather like a helicopter (Puchkov actually tried to build a helicopter before he <u>embarked</u> on this scheme), is all the more remarkable for having been built in total secrecy at the height of the Soviet <u>regime</u>. When he left the army in 1981, Puchkov, now 40, spent six years <u>painstakingly</u> putting it together in his spare time while he worked in a factory in Ryazan, his home town, southeast of Moscow.

He is <u>evasive</u> about where the money came from, though some of the materials he was able to <u>elicit</u> from contacts in the local steel mill. Even his closest friends and family did not know of the existence of the sub, which was kept under a specially constructed cover.

When he was ready, in 1987, he set out along the river Tosna, near Moscow, and managed to sail hundreds of miles as far as the river Neva, which flows through St Petersburg – or Leningrad as it was then known. He was guiding the sub northwards towards the open waters of the Gulf of Finland when it became trapped in a <u>log jam</u> of wood. There was no way to escape, so he was forced to come to the surface; his long-kept secret was out in the open.

'The KGB arrived to arrest me,' Puchkov says. 'They searched the whole submarine for photographs and sent ships to the Gulf of Finland to look for my "accomplices".' The secret service held him in <u>custody</u> for a week; family and friends back home were <u>grilled</u>. 'After a while they worked out that it was all a joke and that I didn't intend to use my sub to spy on anyone.' Then, in an extraordinary <u>volte-face</u>, the authorities sent him to study at a nautical institute in Leningrad. As a result he was offered a job in the navy – which he <u>declined</u>.

Today Puchkov spends October to May working in a glass factory and living in a shared flat. On sunny days he likes to sail to the uninhabited islands in the Gulf of Finland. It isn't all <u>plain sailing</u>: in heavy seas, when the ventilator cannot cope, the overpowering smell of petrol fumes in the cabin makes Puchkov seasick.

But taking risks is part of the thrill for a <u>dare-devil</u>. 'The further out you go, the more frightening it becomes,' he smiles <u>sheepishly</u>. 'There is always the possibility that you won't come back.'

Source: Adapted from Nicholas Brautlecht's article in *The Sunday Times*, 11 February 2001

8 How does the writer of the article convey the impression that he

    a admires Puchkov?
    b does not admire the KGB?

Quote a range of words/phrases from the article and explain their effects.

9 Circle the hyphens, dashes, brackets, colons and semicolons in the article opposite. After discussion with your partner, complete the following sentences to explain the differences between them:

    a *Hyphens, which link two or three words without spaces, are used to...*
    b *They are also used at the end of a line of writing to show that a word...*
    c *Dashes, which are twice the width of hyphens and which have spaces before and after them, are used either singly to ... or as a pair to...*
    d *Brackets are always used in pairs, and they show that...*
    e *Colons indicate that...*
    f *Semicolons perform the role of...*

Your teacher will check your answers.

> ▼ *Exam tip!*
>
> In printed material you will usually find that double inverted commas are not used (as they take more space and make text look cluttered). Instead, singles or italics replace them for speech and titles. In handwriting, however, it is conventional to use double inverted commas for speech so that you can use singles to indicate an ironic usage, a fashionable colloquial expression, a title being referred to within speech, or speech within speech.

10 Sixteen words/phrases are underlined in the article. With your partner, replace them with synonyms. Are there any you could not replace? Look them up in a good dictionary. Add any new words to your personal vocabulary list.

surreal	regime	log jam	declined
bizarre	painstakingly	custody	plain sailing
conventional	evasive	grilled	dare-devil
embarked	elicit	volte-face	sheepishly

11 Using the facts in the 'Mini-sub statistics' box, write three sentences to describe the submarine's appearance and performance, focusing on these characteristics:

    a its dimensions   b its movement   c its power

12 Highlight the facts which give information about Puchkov himself. Write two sentences: (a) giving his life story (b) describing his character.

13 Draw a labelled map, with arrows, to show the journey the submarine made in 1987, using evidence from the text. When you have finished it, compare it with your partner's and evaluate each other's.

14 Summarise the stages in the building and testing of Puchkov's submarine, following the procedure outlined below. Write about one side.

    a   Reread the article and highlight the relevant facts.

    b   Transfer the information, reducing and paraphrasing, to a list, in chronological order.

    c   Group your points logically; link with brackets those which are on the same subject. How many paragraphs would be appropriate?

    d   Express each group of points as one complex sentence (using connectives or participles, varying the ordering of clauses). For example:

       After the Russian had built the frame, he put in the engine, which he had found...

    e   Check your piece of writing. Is it about the right length, legible, complete, correct?

Your partner will mark your summary out of 20 (15 for content, 5 for style) and write a comment on it. A high mark means that all the relevant information has been used, and that it has been expressed concisely, in your own words, and with complete focus on the question.

15 Tell your teacher anything you know about the island of Crete, the mythological character Daedalus or the history of human-powered flight. Then read the account below.

The Daedalus flight

Following the successful capture of the Kremer prize in 1984, the MIT design team began to prepare for their ultimate challenge – the re-enactment of Daedalus' flight from Crete. Preparations were extraordinary. To build and test the 70-pound aircraft took 15,000 hours and one million dollars. Five athletes – bicycling champions – were selected and put through rigorous training and endurance tests. The pilot of the craft would pedal a mechanism which operated through two gear boxes and turned an 11-foot, superlight propeller to provide thrust for the craft. The length of the flight and low speed required that the operator maintain a high level of pedalling power for nearly five hours – not unlike running two back-to-back marathons. Even a new beverage was developed for the flight to replace the perspiration and minerals sweated off by the pilot.

Finally, at 7.06 a.m. on a sunny Saturday last April, the ultralight Daedalus 88 was propelled down the runway of an airfield in Heraklion, Crete, bound for the volcanic island of Santorini 74 miles away. The pilot and 'power' of the plane was Kanellos Kanellopoulos, 31, winner of 14 Greek national cycling championships. Aided by a mild tailwind, the plane advanced at a graceful 18.9 miles per hour. Just three hours and 54 minutes after takeoff, the craft approached the beach of Santorini. Suddenly an offshore gust caught the craft bringing it up into a stall and snapping off its tail. The Daedalus plunged into the sea 30 feet from shore. Undaunted, Kanellopoulos swam to shore, the holder of three world human-power flight records.

Source: Adapted from http://www.yale.edu

16 Underline unfamiliar words in the account (no more than 10) and discuss their meanings with your partner, guessing according to context, or looking them up in a dictionary if necessary.

17 Scan the account and highlight the key facts.

    a Summarise the information in a short paragraph.

    b Reduce the paragraph to one complex sentence.

    c If you have used *and* as a connective, replace it with another connective or use a participle.

Now read your final sentence to the class, who will call out if they think it is not really one sentence. Semicolons are cheating!

18 Write a conversation between Mikhail Puchkov and Kanellos Kanellopoulos. They should explain what motivated them, describe the problems they encountered at various stages and describe how they feel about their achievements. Write about one and a half sides, allowing for the size of your handwriting.

Start like this:

Puchkov: *Personally, I've always been fascinated by the sea.*

Kanellopoulos:

19 Read the following two passages (below and on page 120), which are both about great white sharks.

Text A

Scientists say precious little is known about the more than 370 species of sharks, which evolved over 400 million years ago and have changed little since. Most sharks are less than 90 centimetres long and pose no threat to humans. They can, however, reach more than 6 metres in length and weigh more than 4 tonnes. The most famous and feared of them all is the great white. Great whites are found in nearly every ocean and sea on earth, but their populations are sparse so observing them is extremely difficult. No accurate population estimates exist, but they are categorised as threatened animals because of the decline in the species due to overfishing. People kill more than 100 million sharks per year, mostly for culinary delicacies or their skin. They are protected in the waters off Australia, South Africa and the United States. However, they are often killed as by-products of fishing nets and lines set for other species. Like most sharks, great whites take years to mature and reproduce slowly. They have never been successfully maintained in captivity. Scientists say the myths about sharks should be replaced with scientific facts and that shark attacks are very rare, on average 54 per year worldwide.

Source: *Cyprus Weekly*, 31 August 2001

Text B

The great white shark is a skilled hunter that preys chiefly upon other sea creatures. Negative and exaggerated reporting of the rare shark attacks on humans – not to mention the *Jaws* film effect – have led to the great white and other sharks being deliberately targeted for sports fishing. Rising demand for shark skins, fins, meat and other body parts has led to a boom in their slaughter. The world's population of the great white cannot sustain this hunting, especially when coupled with the threats from fishing nets and pollution. As sharks are at the top of the marine food chain, their slaughter – perhaps as many as 100 million a year – has severe repercussions for the whole marine ecosystem.

Source: *WWF News*, spring 1999

20 With your partner, divide Text A into short paragraphs using the symbol //.

21 Write a summary of (a) the present and (b) the possible future problems facing the great white shark. Use information from Texts A and B. Write about three-quarters of a side.

> ▼ *Exam tip!*
>
> When collating information from more than one source, delete any repetition of facts. Mix the material logically, so that you don't treat the two sources separately but create a seamless response to the task. Follow the structure and number of paragraphs implied in the wording of the task instruction (e.g. in Exercise 21, one paragraph on present problems, another paragraph on future problems).

22 Read the text below describing the way of life of the Incas of Peru.

The Incas

Incas, like the ancient Egyptians, had occult knowledge through which they wrought miracles of engineering. Their cities, their roads, their stonemasonry are astonishing. What was the purpose of that strange network of lines that runs for miles across the plateau surface? What was the meaning of the giant figures, the monkey, the whale and the humming bird, designed to be seen only from the air? How did this desert people, who mummified their dead, know the precise anatomy of a spider found only in the distant forests of Amazonia? For them the birds, the plants, even the very stones harboured spirits.

Inca houses had no locks, no bolts, no proper doors even. There were no thieves, because a benign state provided everything. Money, writing, the arch and the wheel did not exist. Environmentally friendly farming, based on sophisticated terraced systems in the deep Andean valleys, provided for the needs of all. Pizarro and his 130 heavily armoured cavalry destroyed the economy. Or rather the Spaniards who followed him did, driven by the lust for gold. But the Inca jigsaw foundations have withstood everything that nature can throw at them. They still stand, an art form in their own right, as silent tributes to the skills of unknown stonemasons, to the unique survival of the Incas.

The Peruvians claim the magnificent site of Machu Picchu as the eighth wonder of the world. But Machu Picchu is overrun by tourists. It is in danger of becoming a modern theme park. The manicured lawns provide rest for exhausted back-packers who have just completed the Inca Trail. Gardeners work restoring walls and cultivating the terraces. Present-day Peru displays all the problems of a growing country. The modern myth is that history, perhaps, holds the key to their solution.

Source: Adapted from *Cyprus Weekly*, 31 August 2001

23 Ten words are underlined in the passage opposite. Look up any which are unfamiliar, and add them to your personal vocabulary list.

24 How does the writer of the passage opposite convey admiration for the Inca civilisation through the use of stylistic features and vocabulary choices? Give five examples of each and explain their effects.

Navel of the universe

Cuzco, which is 3,600 metres above sea level, was among the greatest wonders of the ancient New World. For the Incas it was literally the sacred centre of the universe. Accordingly they lavished enormous resources on opulent construction and extravagant embellishment. Cuzco and its environs were the quintessence of Inca corporate construction and architecture. Only the finest stonework was used, employing precisely carved blocks that fitted together without the need of cement. Each multi-sided stone was a unique work laboriously cut to a special size and faceted shape that would fit the angles of the adjoining blocks. Two styles of masonry were used for two different classes of structures: polygonal blocks for solid structures, such as terraces and platforms; and ashlar blocks for buildings with freestanding walls and open interior space, often surmounting solid structures. The doors, windows, and niches of Inca buildings were distinctly trapezoidal, being wider at the bottom than at the top. Roofs were gabled and of thatch. Covered buildings ranged from vast assembly halls to small rectangular quarters.

People generally worked out of doors near their small dwellings, and the surrounding enclosure defined their private space. Although Inca architecture and masonry drew on earlier traditions, the lords of Cuzco added their own corporate stamp, transforming their imperial heartland into a majestic parkland. From each of the distant four quarters of Tahuantinsuyu a great highway converged on the central plaza. The navel of the universe, the *capac usnu*, was a multifaceted dais of finely hewn rock with a vertical pillar and a carved seat, which stood within the plaza. The jutting pillar was a celestial sighting point for tracking heavenly luminaries and dark constellations in the quarters of the universe. The sculpted seat was a stone throne where the emperor, the 'son of the sun', maintained terrestrial order. The lord of the realm ascended the dais to review processions, to toast the gods, and to placate the ancestors.

The organising principles of Cuzco were largely misunderstood by the *conquistadores* who left but five short, eyewitness records of the capital before it was consumed by flames during the native rebellion of 1535. These accounts are often contradictory and scholars differ in their interpretations of them. Some scholars argue that the imperial metropolis was designed and laid out in plan as a vast puma. Others deny this. What the Incas had in mind is not clear, but the outline of a great cat seen from the side can be imposed over the architectural tracery of the Inca city. The main plaza creates an open space between the uphill front quarters of the cat, and its rear legs and downhill tail. The head of the cat was formed by the largest and highest edifices, called Sacsahuaman.

Perched atop a high hill, one side of the complex ran along a cliff with a commanding view of the city. The opposite side of the hill was relatively low and encased by three successively higher zigzag terraces. Each wall employed the finest and most impressive of Inca polygonal masonry, including individual stone blocks weighing from 90 to more than 120 metric tons. Excavations have revealed a complex system of finely cut stone channels and drains suggesting ritual manipulation of water. Construction supposedly employed 30,000 workers, who laboured for several generations.

Source: Adapted from Michael Mosley, *The Incas and Their Ancestors*, Thames and Hudson, London, 1992

25 Read the description of the ancient Inca site of Cuzco on page 121.

26 Quote examples of the writer's choice of vocabulary, grammar and sentence structure in the passage on page 121, and comment on the effect of this style.

▼ Exam tip!

Non-fiction informative texts (e.g. passages on historical or scientific topics) are written in the formal style appropriate for textbooks. You can expect to find passive verbs, complex sentences and technical/sophisticated vocabulary, all of which contribute to the impression that the writer is a mature, knowledgeable, trustworthy authority on the subject and that the information is purely factual and unbiased.

---

27 Highlight information from both passages on pages 120 and 121 about the culture, architecture and technology of the Incas.

Use your selected and collated material, in your own words, in an application letter to an educational travel organisation for funding to visit Inca sites in Peru. Explain why you think these sites are worth visiting, and what interests you about the Inca civilisation. Write between one and a half and two sides.

Further practice

a Write notes, in your own words, taken from the boxed passage below, for each of the following summary titles:

   i   *Human attitudes to wolves*
   ii *Why wolves are beneficial to the environment*
   iii *How the relationship with wolves can be improved*

Wolves have been persecuted for centuries. Human attitudes will determine whether our top predators can survive in Europe in the twenty-first century. Most Europeans have lost the traditional knowledge of how to cope with large carnivores and of how humans and predators can coexist. Local people can actually benefit from working with carnivores. By promoting eco-tourism, a country's tourist industry can be extended. Understandably, there is concern about livestock casualties, but throughout history shepherds have effectively used traditional guarding methods with dogs, and sheep and cattle have been protected by being put in pens at night. Public awareness is needed to counteract the view of wolves as wicked, cunning and merciless. This negative image is fuelled by popular mythology and children's stories, and is based on fear rather than fact. Wolves are actually social, timid animals that avoid contact with humans. Wolf attacks on people are extremely rare, but shedding their bloodthirsty reputation involves public education on many levels. These include educational visits, publicity in the international media and the distribution of literature.

---

b Look at the meteorological chart below. Analyse and organise
   the data in it. Write a weather forecast script for television or
   radio of between one and one and a half sides. Express yourself
   clearly and with the minimum of repetition of vocabulary and
   grammatical structures.

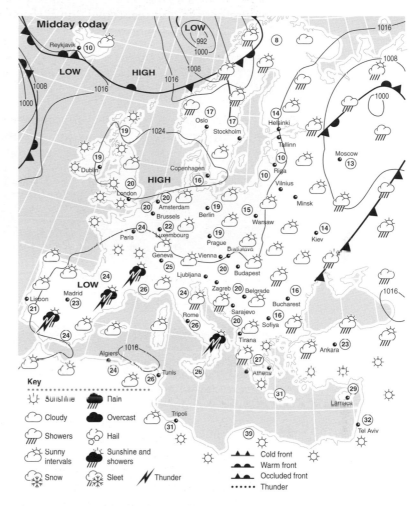

Source: Adapted from *The Guardian*

c Choose a recent technological development which interests you,
   e.g. wireless laptops, interactive digital TV, third-generation
   mobile phones. Research information about how it works and
   what its perceived benefits are. Write a one-side, two-part
   summary using the material you have collected.

Unit 14: *Directed writing*

This unit practises argumentative and discursive responses to texts, and selecting suitable material for reports and articles.

1 Do you believe some people are luckier than others? Do you believe you are a lucky or an unlucky person?

Discuss this topic as a class. Notice which students sound more convincing when they express their views, and why.

Do members of your class, on the whole, believe in luck or not?

2 Read the newspaper article opposite on the subject of luck.

3 Express the following phrases from the article in your own words. You may need to refer to a dictionary. Compare your answers with your partner's and decide which is better in each case.

 a *the masters of our own destinies*
 b *to land on their feet*
 c *all sorts of adversities*
 d *triumph of nurture over nature*
 e *drift into a life of crime*

Scientists prove that we make our own luck

BORN LUCKY? Probably not. Scientists undertaking the biggest study yet into the role luck plays in people's lives say that we are almost certainly the masters of our own destinies.

Researchers from the Institute of Child Health at Bristol University have begun a study of 14,000 children to try to discover whether we are ruled by fate or can create our own luck.

Over the next two years the children will be asked a series of questions about self-esteem, achievement and the role of luck. Researchers will use this to try to ascertain why some people always seem to land on their feet.

'Some people cope with all sorts of adversities and we want to find out why,' said Professor Jean Goulding, the project director.

Steve Nowicki, a clinical psychologist and visiting professor at Emory University, Atlanta, who will play a key role in the study, has been working on the subject for 30 years and believes he already knows the answer. His work suggests that luck is a triumph of nurture over nature and that people's personalities influence how they are treated by fate.

He believes that, when confronted by a problem, people fall into two groups: internalists and externalists. 'Internalists analyse, act and learn from whatever the outcome is. Externalists believe they have no control over their fate and they are passive. If they fall over, they just blame bad fortune instead of trying to work out why and how to prevent it happening again.'

The willingness of externalists to see the hand of fate in what has happened makes them liable to more 'bad luck'. Nowicki's research suggests they are more likely to drift into a life of crime than internalists, who tend to become high achievers.

Which group a child grows into depends most importantly on the influence of parents, grandparents, teachers and peers. Nowicki suggests children from rich backgrounds are more likely to become externalists than children from poor backgrounds, who have had to overcome adversity to succeed.

Source: Adapted from *The Sunday Times,* 17 June 2001

4 Write a discursive response to the article above, in which you present the different views on the existence of luck to readers of a teenage magazine.

Refer to the internalist/externalist theory mentioned in the article, and any other relevant material which is stated or can be inferred. As support use examples from your own experience and from the class discussion in Exercise 1, as well as from the text. Write between one and a half and two sides.

> ▼ *Exam tip!*
>
> Coursework assignment 3 must be based on a text containing 'facts, opinions and arguments'. Candidates are required to respond to the text by 'selecting, analysing and evaluating points from the material'. When you answer, examine the thinking behind the reading material. It may be better to disagree than to agree. Use one, or at most two, articles, neither of them unduly long.

5 Write an argumentative response to the article above, in which you express to Steve Nowicki your own views on his opinions and research.

6 Share around the class the reading aloud of the three news reports on pages 126 and 127. They concern alleged sightings of a Monkey Man in India.

Text A
Monkey mystery baffles Delhi

Police in the Indian capital Delhi are still on the trail of a mysterious creature which has allegedly attacked the city's residents.

The creature, which is described as part man, part monkey, has apparently struck in 65 locations and has led to the deaths of at least two people.

In the absence of solid fact, and fuelled by intense media attention and lurid descriptions, the 'man–monkey' has spread panic in parts of Delhi.

Police say they have been flooded with panic calls, not all of which are genuine.

'Altogether we received about 100 distress calls but only 16 attacks could be verified,' Suresh Roy, the deputy commissioner of police, said on Thursday.

'Eighteen people have been injured since last night. We cannot yet say who, or what, is causing these attacks,' he said.

'Nocturnal beast'

The attacks have taken place at night, and have targeted people sleeping on the roofs of their houses to escape the summer heat.

Patrols have been stepped up in areas where the creature has been sighted, with police manning rooftops.

But their job has been made harder with the wildly varying descriptions of the creature. It is said to be anything between a tiny man to a tall beast – some say with metal claws.

'When I grabbed it, it turned into a cat with glowing eyes,' one resident, who claimed to have encountered the creature, said.

'It looks like a monkey and has green lights as eyes and springs on its feet. It has a huge metallic silver hand which glows in the dark,' he said.

Rumours dismissed

The event has made the front-pages of the capital's daily newspapers, which have even published police sketches of the mysterious creature.

But animal experts rejected the notion that the creature was a primate of any sort.

'I am 120% sure they are humans,' primatologist Iqbal Malick told the AFP news agency.

'These are most definitely pranksters who are getting kicks out of their jokes and, in the process, giving monkeys a bad name,' she said.

Delhi is home to the rhesus monkey which has become a menace in recent times, attacking bureaucrats in government ministries and tearing files and documents.

Source: http://news.bbc.co.uk

Text B

'Monkey Man' sows panic in India's Rajasthan

JAIPUR, India (Reuters) – Less than a week after a mysterious 'monkey man' triggered panic in the Indian capital, panic gripped the northwestern state of Rajasthan where villagers said they had been attacked by a similar looking creature.

But police said people in the desert state's Nagaur district had been attacked on Monday by a wild cat that strayed into people's homes to escape the blistering heat. Local police have sought the help of forest officials to track down the animal.

Last week, parts of New Delhi were terrorised by reports of a marauding 'monkey man' that attacked people in the city of 13 million at random. But New Delhi police said their investigations showed that the 'monkey man' was neither man nor monkey but a result of public hysteria.

Descriptions of the nocturnal 'monkey man' varied wildly with some saying it was a monkey-like creature with metallic claws and others saying it was like a cat with tawny, glowing eyes.

Police in New Delhi said they were also looking into the possibility that criminals or pranksters may have been involved in the scare in which three people plunged to their deaths from buildings because they thought the 'monkey man' was chasing them.

The first reported attack of the 'monkey man' was on April 8 in the neighbouring state of Uttar Pradesh and reports of the creature later spread to Delhi. At the height of the panic in Delhi, vigilante groups armed with sticks patrolled the streets at night on the lookout for the creature.

Police have announced a 50,000 rupee ($1,000) reward for information leading to the capture of the 'monkey man'.

Source: *Cyprus Review*, 25 May 2001 © Reuters Limited 2001 (adapted)

Text C

Indian police release pictures of Monkey Man killer

Indian police have issued pictures of the Monkey Man killer, amid reports he has claimed his second victim.

ABHIMANYU

A pregnant woman died after falling down stairs at her East Delhi home as her family fled from the creature.

Officers in Ghaziabad are offering to pay £75 to anyone who can capture the Monkey Man on film. Around 1,000 officers are involved in the search.

Vigilantes are taking to the streets frustrated at the police's failure to catch him.

In Noida, a mechanic wearing a black outfit and fitting a description of the Monkey Man was beaten up. A second man was attacked for apparently performing 'mystical formulations'.

Some witnesses say the failure to capture the Monkey Man is explained by his ability to make himself invisible.

Deepali Kumari, from Noida, said: 'It has three buttons on its chest. One makes it turn into a monkey, the second gives it extra strength, the third makes it invisible.

'He touches a lock and it breaks. But he is afraid of the light.'

Source: http://www.ananova.com

7 Discuss as a class what you have noticed about the following:

    a the content of the three reports
    b the quality of expression in each of them
    c the different headlines

8 Highlight in each of the three reports, in different colours, both facts and opinions concerning the situation. Compare your selections with your partner's.

9 Agree with your partner on answers to the following questions about the reports:

    a Which report contains most facts?
    b Which report contains most opinions?
    c Which one did you find most convincing?
    d Which one did you find most entertaining?

10 Write an article for a news magazine in which you express your reactions to the 'Monkey Man' story. Give your article a suitable title.

Use the facts and opinions from Texts A and B. Change the information into your own words and order and collate material from both sources without repetition. You should also add material which can be inferred from the reports and the illustrations. Write between one and a half sides and two sides.

▼ *Exam tip!*

Unlike a news report, whose aim is informative, a magazine article comments on a topical situation and is discursive or argumentative. Paragraphs, though still short by comparison with other kinds of writing, are longer in an article than in a report, and the facts are expressed in a less condensed way; e.g. in a news report you might say *36-year-old ex-schoolteacher and mother of two, Margaret Smith, says…*, whereas in an article it might be *Margaret Smith, who is in her mid-thirties, has two children, and used to be a teacher in a junior school, believes that…*

---

11 Read the three Internet texts below, opposite and on page 130, which deal with recent discoveries about dinosaurs in Argentina.

Text A
'Jurassic Park' unearthed in Argentina

Buenos Aires, Argentina (Reuters) – Argentine palaeontologists have announced the discovery of a sprawling 'Jurassic Park' of dinosaur fossils in the heart of Patagonia, which they dubbed 'possibly the most significant find ever'.

The find in the province of Chubut, on an arid plateau some 1,500 km south of Buenos Aires, includes four unknown species of dinosaur from the Jurassic period around 150–160 million years ago.

Experts estimated they had unearthed only around two per cent of the contents of the vast fossil deposit, which sprawls over hundreds of square kilometres in southern Argentina.

Gerardo Cladera of the Egidio Feruglio Palaeontology Museum in Trelew, whose team of experts made the find, said, 'Jurassic-period fossils are very, very rare. They have only been found in China and Madagascar, so we know very little about the evolution of the dinosaurs from this key period.'

'High sea levels during the tropical Jurassic period – which extended from 213 to 144 million years ago – meant there was relatively little land on which dinosaur remains could remain intact, and not be washed away into the oceans,' Cladera added.

The new species found – which the experts have yet to classify and name – include two herbivorous sauropodi some 10 metres long, and larger carnivorous theropodi. One of the sauropoda fossils was also believed to be complete, something very rare for dinosaur remains.

Argentina is renowned for its dinosaur finds. The province of Neuquen, southwest of Buenos Aires, was a steaming swamp millions of years ago and has been dubbed 'Dinosaur Valley' thanks to the myriad fossils found there. It also yielded the remains of the largest dinosaur known to have roamed the earth, the Argentinosaurus, discovered in 1990.

The latest discovery in the area of Chubut was made when a local farmer found bones emerging from a rock on the plain. The Trelew team will start excavating the remains at the beginning of March.

Source: *Cyprus Review*, 23 February 2001 © Reuters Limited 2001 (adapted)

Text B

Group of Giganotosaurus found

4–5 giant meat-eaters in Argentina
April 15, 1998

Rodolfo Coria and Phillip Currie have excavated four or five Giganotosaurus fossils of different sizes in the Patagonian plains of Argentina. Two of the specimens are very large, the others are smaller. They date from 90 million years ago, during the Cretaceous period. The site was discovered by a local goat-herd. Coria, a palaeontologist from the Carmen Funes Museum in Neuquen, Argentina, described the original Giganotosaurus in 1993. Currie is the curator of the Royal Tyrrell Museum of Palaeontology in Drumheller, Alberta, Canada.

Giganotosaurus was a carnivorous dinosaur even larger than T. rex. Because of its very small brain case, it had been thought that Giganotosaurus was a relatively dumb dinosaur, exhibiting few complex behaviours. The existence of a pack of these dinosaurs shows that these assumptions may have been too simplistic. Social behaviour on the part of Giganotosaurus (suggested by finding individuals of different sizes in the group) means that it was smarter than previously thought, perhaps cooperating while hunting and/or protecting the young. On the other hand, the dinosaurs may have simply been gathering at a waterhole at the time of their demise.

Giga-noto-saurus means 'giant southern reptile'. Giganotosaurus was originally found by a local auto mechanic whose hobby is hunting dinosaur bones. In honour of the discoverer, Ruben Carolini, the huge dinosaur has been named Giganotosaurus carolinii. Its fossil was unearthed in the Patagonia region of southeastern Argentina (near the town of El Chocon) in 1993. 70 per cent of the skeleton has been found. Near the Giganotosaurus, fossils were found of a 75-foot-long sauropod (plant eater), Argentinosaurus, presumably a victim of Giganotosaurus.

Source: http://www.enchantedlearning.com

Text C
A comparison of Giganotosaurus and Tyrannosaurus rex

	GIGANOTOSAURUS carolinii	TYRANNOSAURUS rex
Skull length	6 feet (1.8 m)	5 feet (1.5 m)
Hands	3 fingers	larger, with 2 fingers
Height at hips	12 feet (3.7 m)	10 feet (3 m)
Length	45–47 feet (14.5 m)	40 feet (12 m)
Weight	about 8 tons	about 5 tons
Teeth	long, knife-like, serrated – slicing action	conical, serrated – crushing action
Brain size, shape	small, banana shaped	larger and wider
When they lived	about 100–95 million years ago	about 68–65 million years ago
Where they lived	South America	North America

Giganotosaurus

Giganotosaurus was a 47-foot-long meat-eating dinosaur which weighed about 8 tons and stood 12 feet tall (at the hips). It walked on two legs, had a brain the size of a banana, and had enormous jaws with 8-inch-long, knife-like, serrated teeth in a 6-foot-long skull. Giganotosaurus was a theropod from the mid-Cretaceous period, living about 100–95 million years ago, toward the end of the Mesozoic era, the 'Age of Reptiles'.

Although some news sources (like Reuters) reported that Giganotosaurus kept T. rex from venturing into South America, this is wrong. Giganotosaurus lived and died millions of years before T. rex evolved. Also, a sea separated North and South America during the Cretaceous period. These two titans could never have met, unless they had a time machine and a boat.

Source: http://www.enchantedlearning.com

 Look at the boxes in Text C again, then reread Texts A and B, highlighting facts about the different types of dinosaur and being careful not to duplicate anything. Check that you have not highlighted any facts contained in the boxes.

Suggest facts to your teacher to put on the board.

 Circle the punctuation used to create parentheses in the three texts – i.e. commas, dashes and brackets – which are used in pairs to separate an embedded phrase or clause from the rest of the sentence.

Discuss with your partner what you think the difference is between the three types. Tell your teacher what you have concluded.

14 Imagine you have been asked to give a talk to a school science club on recent dinosaur finds in Argentina. Use your highlighted material from Exercise 11, (a) to support the belief in the existence of a new species of dinosaur discovered in 1993 and (b) to present the case for its having lived in a different period from Tyrannosaurus rex.

Write between one and a half and two sides. (Practise using different types of parentheses in your sentence structures, as well as colons and semicolons.)

Further practice

a   Find a report of an event or comments published in a national or local newspaper or magazine on a topic about which you have a strong view. Write to the letters page of the newspaper or magazine to present your argument. Remember to use evidence to support your case and to refer to the original report or article. Write one and a half sides. Begin *Dear Editor...*

b   A group of parents has raised some money to finance an arts event at your school. The three possibilities are described in the boxes below. They would all cost about the same.

A. Classical musical recital of works by Beethoven and Chopin performed by renowned foreign pianist – open to the public – subsidised entry charge – to take place over two consecutive evenings	B. Touring theatre group – good reputation – to perform a modern version of 'Romeo and Juliet' – literature exam set text – whole school may attend – taking place at end of school day – free entry	C. Local poet in school for the day – readings, workshops, competitions – students off timetable for the day – only one year group can be involved – has visited school previously and day was a success

Imagine you are the Head of the Arts Faculty in your school. You have been asked to write to the chair of the parents' group explaining which of these events you think would most benefit the education of the students.

Write about two sides in which you include
- the reasons why you think all school arts events are desirable
- comments on all three possibilities
- your preference and the reasons for your choice

c Using the statistics on multiple births below, write an analytical report on the topic as an introduction to a research project for biology coursework. Think carefully about a structure for your writing. You should mention
- changes over time in the UK and future implications
- differences between countries
- different kinds of multiple births

Multiple birth rate in the UK (number of sets)

Year	Twins	Triplets	Quads and more	Total	Per 1,000 births
1982	6,201	70	6	6,277	10.07
1983	6,239	89	5	6,387	10.20
1984	6,321	80	5	6,406	10.10
1985	6,700	93	10	6,803	10.42
1986	6,969	123	13	7,105	10.81
1987	7,186	125	9	7,320	10.80
1988	7,452	157	13	7,622	11.06
1989	7,579	183	12	7,774	11.38
1990	7,934	201	1	8,145	11.62
1991	8,160	208	12	8,380	12.08
1992	8,314	202	9	8,525	12.47
1993	8,302	234	13	8,549	12.79
1994	8,451	260	8	8,719	13.22

Fraternal (non-identical) twin rates
Japan: 6 per 1,000 births (1 in 166)
Nigeria: 45 per 1,000 (1 in 22)
USA: 11 per 1,000 (1 in 90)

Identical twin rates
3.5 per 1,000 (1 in 285) (Universal figure)

Conjoined twin rates
1 in 50,000

Overall twin rates
China: 1 in 250
Japan: 1 in 150
Nigeria: 1 in 22
Norway, Denmark, Netherlands: 1 in 49
UK: 1 in 76
USA: White Americans: 1 in 69
        Black Americans: 1 in 60

Unit 15: *Composition*

This unit looks at the appropriate content and style for presenting an argument or discussion in exam compositions or coursework. We also give advice about spelling.

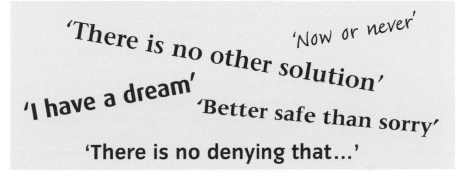

'There is no other solution'   'Now or never'

'I have a dream'   'Better safe than sorry'

'There is no denying that…'

❶ To get you in the mood for arguing, practise with paragraph-length speeches. Choose one topic from the list below, plan in your head what you are going to say, then tell the rest of the class your opinion:

- the best day of the week
- the most satisfying food
- the most entertaining television programme
- the perfect holiday
- the ideal friend

> **▼** *Exam tip!*
>
> If you enjoy giving an opinion and can express yourself clearly, consider choosing an argument title as an IGCSE Composition task or for coursework. Remember the difference between discursive writing (looking at a topic from various points of view) and argumentative writing (taking a particular position on an issue and presenting a case for its being the only correct view). Your own personal view is the position you are likely to argue most convincingly. However, you may be asked to argue on a subject you have not considered before or about which you have no particular view, and you will still need to sound convincing!

❷ You and your partner disagree completely! One of you will argue for and one will argue against the response to one of the moral dilemmas listed below. The class will vote on who is the more convincing in each pair.

Your teacher will tell you which one to prepare and perform. Begin either *Yes, because…* or *No, because…*

a   You know your friend has cheated in their coursework by downloading a composition from the Internet. Do you tell anyone about your discovery?

b   You knock over and break an ornament at a relative's house. Do you blame the cat?

c   You are given too much change for a purchase in a shop. Do you tell the assistant and return the extra money?

d   You caused slight damage to a parked car with your bicycle. Do you leave a note with your name and address?

e   You see someone shoplifting whom you know slightly. Do you tell the shop owner?

f   Your parents think you did well in recent school exams, because there was a mistake in the grade on the report. Do you tell them the truth?

g   It is possible for you to pay less than you should for a train journey by lying about which station you came from. Do you?

h   You find a wallet in the street containing some money and an address. Do you contact the owner?

i   You did not do your homework because you went out with your friends instead. Do you tell your teacher the real reason for not doing it?

j   You try on a new garment when you get home from the shop and you spill something on it. Do you take it back and ask for a free replacement, claiming that the stain was already there?

❸ You use argument every day in a variety of contexts, some of which you can work out from Exercise 2. With your partner, list all the different situations you can think of in which people use argument in speech and writing. You have 5 minutes. Two examples have been started.

A teacher in a classroom uses argument to…

An election candidate at a public meeting uses argument to…

Share your answers with the class. Which pair got the most?

❹ Read the newspaper article on page 135, written by a doctor.

❺ This article expresses the writer's personal and professional view on the subject of health. With your partner, do the following tasks:

a   Highlight phrases or sentences that identify the argument being developed in the article. These are sometimes called 'topic sentences' (although they do not need to be complete sentences), or 'topic headings'.

b   Give the article a title that indicates the view being expressed.

c   List all the methods used to win the reader's attention and agreement, giving examples. One example has been provided.

strong vocabulary – 'deranged', 'obsession'

The outer person is not...

OVER the past decade we've all become more health conscious, but in doing so we seem to have perverted the meaning of health. Health is no longer something everyone is born with and retains if they are lucky. Health is a commodity. It is something you can have more of. And to qualify for this extra health you have to buy a tracksuit, eat vitamin pills, have a therapist and learn to do one-handed press-ups.

This all sounds quite harmless, until you realise it implies that people who are not perfectly formed, who are not young, sporty and suntanned, are less valuable people. We all want to be healthy, but we should perhaps come down off the exercise bike and clarify what the word health actually means.

For a start, health is not beauty and fitness. You can have wonderful hair and huge muscles, while your internal organs are in a terrible state.

The outer person is not a direct reflection of the inner person. If life were that simple, medical diagnosis would be an awful lot easier.

Second, health is not a purely physical state. It's mental as well. There are lots of supremely fit people who are psychologically deranged and, conversely, a lot of quite seriously disabled people who are bright, happy and perfectly in tune with themselves. Compulsive slimming and exercising are a form of obsession, and obsession is a form of mental illness.

Besides, the criteria for physical and mental health are a matter of opinion, containing a strong social element. In any society except his own, Attila the Hun would have been regarded as a psychopath. There's a tribe in the Amazon rainforest which regards you as unwell if you don't have pale, circular patches of fungal infection on your skin.

Taking all this into account, health is a terribly difficult word to define. It is nevertheless important to do so, because unless we know what health is we don't know what to aim for. Enshrined in the constitution of the World Health Organization is this statement: 'Health is a state of complete physical, mental and social well-being, and not merely the absence of disease or infirmity.' Arguably, this says it all, but it makes a nonsense of the WHO's proclaimed objective to provide health for all by the year 2000.

My own favourite definition of health is 'psychological health is the ability to love and to work'. It's an easy thing to aim for and at the same time very difficult to arrive at. There are, however, occasional moments in everyone's life when you experience, simultaneously, a great love for those around you and also a great sense of personal fulfilment. These fleeting moments are very hard to achieve, but they constitute a more worthwhile aim in life than trying to look like Jane Fonda.

Source: Adapted from John Collee, *The Observer*, 30 December 1990

▼ *Exam tip!*   *relates to Exercises 4 and 5*

Notice the use of first and second person (*I*, *we* and *you*) in the article in Exercise 4. Personal references and direct appeals can be used in your own arguments to create a relationship with the reader, but you should balance them with facts, statistics and dates, which give the impression of knowledge and objectivity, whether true or not! The media are a useful source of topical examples to support your view. Exaggeration for conveying ridicule and creating humour can also be an effective method of securing reader interest, sympathy and support.

6 *Health is a terribly difficult word to define.* How would you define health? Do you think people generally are more or less healthy than they used to be? What about the future of medicine? Can and should disease be eradicated? How do you feel about the state of hospitals and the medical profession nowadays? How have attitudes to health changed over time?

a Write a plan for a discursive composition called *Health*. You need at least eight separate ideas or points to cover a range of views and aspects. Put them in order.

b Experiment with possible first sentences for the composition.

c Ask your partner to choose the best, justifying the choice.

7 Discuss with your partner the weaknesses of the following openings for argument titles. (The titles are given in brackets.)

a *Water has many uses.* (*Water is life*)

b *As with most questions, there are two sides to be considered.* (*Capital punishment*)

c *Nobody who has a television could have not been horrified by the recent events.* (*What are your views on the invention of television?*)

d *Many factors affect how we live today.* (*Does life get better or worse?*)

e *I feel very very strongly about this topic.* (*Is there such a thing as justice?*)

▼ *Exam tip!*

The first sentence of any writing, but especially argument, is very important for engaging the reader. An obvious or dull statement will not arouse interest in the topic or inspire confidence in your opinions. An effective opening could be

• an unexpected claim – e.g. *Technology is making humans more primitive.*

• a provocative statement – e.g. *We all lose control sometimes.*

• a succinct summary of a situation – e.g. *Global warming is responsible for most of the earth's environmental problems.*

• a famous quotation – e.g. *All power corrupts, and absolute power corrupts absolutely.*

• a direct question – e.g. *How do you feel about the world your children will inherit?*

Which type of opening is used in the article in Exercise 4?

---

8 Using the suggestions for openings in the exam tip above, agree with your partner on more effective ways to start the compositions in Exercise 7. Share your ideas with the rest of the class.

9 Identify and list the words/phrases used to link paragraphs in the article in Exercise 4. Two examples are provided:

This

For a start

What other words/phrases can be used to link paragraphs? With your partner, add as many more as you can.

Structure is essential in argumentative writing; there should be a sense of logical development in the order of your points, and a connection between paragraphs. Common linking words/phrases are *therefore, furthermore, in addition, on the other hand, however, on the contrary, nevertheless*. (Avoid using only a list of numbers, *first, second, third* etc.) The function of these linking phrases is to continue a line of argument or to change its direction. Don't change direction more than once in an argument, or you may confuse the reader. It can be effective to begin your composition by mentioning the opposite view from your own, so that you can then refute it to strengthen your own case, which is developed in the rest of the composition.

❿ Use numbers to put the planning notes below into the most logical and effective order for an argument composition entitled *Money is the root of all evil*. Choose the first and last points especially carefully.

- reason for wars
- responsible for greed and envy
- gives people false values
- not distributed fairly
- gambling an addiction
- connected to politics – causes corruption
- rich people often unhappy
- cause of most crimes – drugs trade
- can destroy relationships

Compare your numbering with that of your partner. If they differ, argue your case.

⓫ Expand the topic headings in Exercise 10 by adding details next to each, including examples, references to people or events, statistics or well-known sayings. Share your suggestions with the class.

⓬ Which linking words/phrases in your answers to Exercise 9 and in the exam tip would be appropriate to use in the planned composition in Exercise 10? Write one in front of each topic heading.

13 The plan in Exercise 10 supports the argument that money has a harmful influence in the world, but it would be equally possible to present a case for its being beneficial.

Plan the opposite point of view silently for five minutes. The title is *Money makes the world go round*. Include the linking words/phrases you would use.

Give your ideas to the teacher to put on the board for class discussion of the best content and order for the composition.

> ▼ *Exam tip!*
>
> Any title set in the exam can be argued from both sides, positive and negative, so if you find you cannot get enough points for the side you first try to plan, think about presenting the alternative case. A planning time of between 5 and 10 minutes is recommended for an exam composition, and there is no time limit for coursework planning. Remember it is not your views that are being judged, but your ability to construct a relevant, varied, linked composition in an appropriate style and effective order for the title and type of writing you have chosen.

14 Read the text below, which is an **editorial** from a national daily newspaper.

Safe landing

Nothing can replace old-fashioned pilot skills

LITTLE can be more terrifying than the sudden silence when the engines cut out at 35,000 feet. Those passengers aboard the Air Transat Airbus over the Atlantic knew the danger they were in; and the panic pounding through the announcements by the crew left them in no doubt that the pilot's attempt to make an emergency landing in the Azores was as risky as the alternative of ditching in the sea. For 65 miles the plane glided towards Lajes military airbase, buffeted by turbulence while holding fast to the descent path that was Captain Robert Piché's single chance of survival. Miraculously, he brought the plane down safely.

Although all planes are designed to glide in emergency, controlling an airliner the size of an A330-200 is no easy task. The pilot has to pitch the plane exactly right, keep it balanced and ensure precise timing. His experience saved him and all his passengers.

Pilot error is often highlighted as the main cause of air crashes nowadays. This gives the wrong impression of the competence and skill of those who fly the giant airliners. Their judgment is only rarely tested in emergency, but pilots in recent years have several times achieved the heroic: landing safely at Manchester airport on only two wheels, gliding an El Salvador plane to safety after a hailstorm disabled the engines and, most famously, landing a DC10 in a cornfield in Iowa after the hydraulic system had been disabled.

In every instance, old-fashioned piloting saved the plane. Nothing can replace this basic training.

Source: Adapted from *The Times*, 27 August 2001

15 Discuss as a class why newspapers have editorials. What sorts of issues do they comment on, and why?

16 With your partner, find rhetorical devices (expressions chosen to influence the reader) in the text in Exercise 14. Find examples of the following:

a words that evoke strong emotion – e.g. *emergency landing*
b words that have dramatic effect – e.g. *terrifying*
c word order for emphasis – e.g. *Nothing can replace*
d alliteration for impact – e.g. *sudden silence*
e words that make clear the view of the writer – e.g. *Miraculously*
f words that express absolutes – e.g. *no doubt*

> ▼ *Exam tip!*
>
> To argue effectively you must be familiar with typical features of **rhetoric** (argument style). In addition to the devices mentioned in Exercise 16, these include
> - triple structures – to emphasise scope or variety (e.g. *Before, during, after the event*)
> - questions – to engage reader (e.g. *Do we really believe that…?*)
> - exclamations – to suggest strong feeling (e.g. *Heaven forbid!*)
> - repetition – to emphasise key idea (e.g. *Education, education, education*)
> - hypotheticals – to make strongest possible case by discussing best- or worst-case scenario (e.g. *If this were to happen* or *Unless we do something*)
> - negatives – to stress difficulty and danger (e.g. *no easy task* or *not one person*)
> - intensifiers – for emphasis (e.g. *only, extremely, absolutely*)
> - lists – to impress with number (e.g. *men, women, children, babies*)
> - elevated diction – to make speaker seem educated (e.g. *eradicate* instead of *get rid of*)
> - **antithesis** – for ironic or dramatic contrast (e.g. *small step for a man, giant leap for mankind*)
>
> Don't use excessively emotive language, however, as there is a danger of your case sounding more like biased **propaganda** than a considered and reasoned opinion based on evidence.

17 With your partner, plan an argument to oppose that expressed by the editorial in Exercise 14, in which you argue that human beings are and always have been the main cause of accidents and disasters, and that machines are generally more reliable. The title is *Human error*.

Decide on your examples and evidence, and the order of your points.

Write your final sentence and read it to the class to judge its effectiveness.

> ▼ *Exam tip!*
>
> Endings should be strong and climactic to clinch your argument. (Think of lawyers summing up in court.) Don't end randomly, fade away or weaken your argument by repetition, and try to avoid such obvious expressions as *In conclusion* or *To sum up*. To conclude effectively, you might
> - refer back to an opening statement
> - look into the future
> - suggest a new angle
> - make an original observation
> - give a short definitive statement
> - quote a famous saying
> - make a humorous comment
>
> Which type of ending is used in the article in Exercise 14?

18 Plan and write your own editorial on anything that is currently in the national or international news. Write about one side.

Give your article a headline, short and clever (refer to the exam tip on headlines in Unit 6 on page 49) and a sub-headline which gives the gist of the argument.

Practise the rhetorical devices mentioned in Exercise 16 and in the exam tip. Read your editorial to the class. It should sound powerful and persuasive as a speech.

19 The words listed below are useful in argument and discussion compositions and coursework.

a Tick the words you already know and use regularly.
b Asterisk the words you use rarely but know the meaning of. Make a mental note to use them more in future.
c Highlight the words you do not use because you are not sure of their meanings. Use a dictionary to check meanings, and add the words to your personal vocabulary list.

acknowledge	exaggerate	phenomenon
acquaintance	excellent	possession
appropriate	existence	prejudice
attempt	experience	privilege
beautiful	extremely	psychological
beginning	foreign	pursue
business	government	receive
campaign	immediately	reminiscent
completely	independent	separate
conscience	interesting	skilful
criticism	irrelevant	specific
decision	necessary	subtle
definitely	noticeable	successful
disappearance	occasionally	surprise
embarrassment	occurred	temporary
enthusiasm	opportunity	thorough
environment	parliament	unique
especially	persuade	vulnerable

20 All the words in the vocabulary list above are often misspelt, even by educated native speakers of English.

a Discuss with your partner why each of the words is difficult to spell.
b Underline the 'hot spot' in each word – i.e. the precise point of difficulty.
c Circle the words whose spelling surprises you, that you have misspelt in the past or that you regularly get wrong.
d Focus on the hot spots in your circled words for 5 seconds each.

e   Test yourself on these words, using the Look-Cover-Write-Check method, which means covering the word while you write it from memory and then comparing your answer with the correct spelling.

f   Learn any words you got wrong by continuing to focus on the 'hot spot' of the correct spelling and retesting until you get them right.

▼ Exam tip!

Although in IGCSE you won't be penalised for misspelling an individual word, accuracy is important in an English language examination; you are unlikely to be awarded the higher grades if your spelling is consistently weak, and sometimes errors can create confusion. Fortunately, you can improve your spelling during the course. Try these strategies:

- Always look up and correct spelling errors in returned work.
- Never guess a spelling you're unsure of; this reinforces errors.
- Don't rely on a computer spellcheck. (They can be misleading.)
- Notice which letter strings are possible in English – e.g. *qu* but never *qi*; *-tion* but not *-toin*.
- Compare with cognate words in other languages, such as French, Greek, Latin or Spanish.
- Create a visual image of the word, using the Look-Cover-Write-Check method.
- Make up **mnemonics**, **acronyms** and rhymes to help you – e.g. *It is necessary for one coat to have two sleeves* (one *c*, double *ss* in *necessary*).
- Group words with silent letters – e.g. *debt/doubt; knot/knob*.
- Find words in other words – e.g. *science* in *conscience; finite* in *definitely*.
- With difficult long words, separate the syllables – e.g. *Wed-nes-day, extra-ordin-ary, inter-esting*.
- Remember that there is a small group of two-syllabled nouns ending in *ce* which end in *se* when they become a verb – e.g. *practice/se; licence/se*.
- Learn rules of thumb:
  - *i* before *e* except after *c*, when you are sounding a long double *ee* (the only exception is *seize* and some names, e.g. *Keith*)
  - double consonant, short vowel; single consonant, long vowel (e.g. *hopping* and *hoping*)
  - adverbs end in *-ly* unless the adjective already ends in *-l*, then it's *-lly* (e.g. *safely* and *successfully*)

Further practice

a   Write your discursive composition entitled *Health*, planned in Exercise 6, or your argumentative composition entitled *Money makes the world go round*, planned in Exercise 13.

b   A book, film or theatre review is a type of argumentative writing. It presents a supported case as to whether or not readers should go out and buy the book or see the film or play. Write a review of something you have read or seen recently. Make it about two sides long and give examples as support.

c   Plan the following argument or discussion titles as exam practice or coursework preparation:

   i   *Do you believe in the supernatural?*
   ii   *Extra-terrestrial life*
   iii   *The role of the artist in today's world.*
   iv   *Vegetarianism*
   v   *Does global communication contribute to global harmonisation?*

Unit 16: *Speaking and listening*

This unit practises coursework role plays and talks, and looks at rhetorical style and delivery in presenting spoken arguments.

❶ Volunteer to read aloud a paragraph of the short text below.

Clouds

What's the weather like where you are? Chances are there's a cloud somewhere on your horizon – a collection of millions of microscopic water droplets formed as moist air rises, cools and expands. If the cloud is dense enough, it rains. If it's cold enough, it snows. And if it's low enough, we call it fog.

But until 200 years ago, people didn't know what to call them and the fluffy things that passed overhead were known by their resemblance to things such as mare's tails or mackerel's scales.

In 1783, huge volcanic eruptions in Iceland and Japan produced spectacular sunsets across the northern hemisphere. Eleven-year-old Luke Howard was entranced by these displays and became a keen student of the young science of meteorology. Twenty years later, he made the first internationally recognised classification of clouds.

Suddenly the sky was full of cirrus (high, threadlike cloud) and stratus (low, layered cloud), nimbus (rainclouds) and cumulus (low, puffy cloud). By combining these Latin names and grouping them by the height at which they occurred, Howard came up with a 10-point system for identifying clouds.

Some countries may be sick of the sight of them, but drought-stricken areas are crying out for a bit of cloud cover. Scientists in the US and Russia have attempted to create clouds by cloud seeding – dropping condensation agents such as dry ice from aeroplanes to encourage nascent clouds to form.

Artists, too, have found inspiration in the skies – Wordsworth wandered lonely as one, Shelley named a poem after 'the daughter of earth and water and the nursling of the sky', while Turner and Constable captured their fleeting likenesses on canvas.

Whether you are under one, on top of one or have your head in one, clouds, like our moods, are ever changing. And perhaps that is the beauty of them.

Source: Adapted from *Times Educational Supplement*, 15 June 2001

❷ Is it possible this could be an impromptu (unprepared) talk on clouds by someone interested in the topic? List in two columns, as below, the evidence for its being a written or a spoken text. Examples have been given.

Written	Spoken
technical language	*contracted forms*

3 The class is going to play a semi-impromptu speaking game. Your teacher has written some noun words/phrases on slips of paper and put them into a box. One by one you will pick a slip at random and spend 2 minutes thinking of what you will say about the subject. You may write very brief notes. A time-keeper will tell you when to begin addressing the class, and the aim is to keep talking for 2 minutes, when you will be stopped.

Use as many relevant ideas as you can think of, give lots of examples, and mix description and information in your presentation. You can be as humorous as you wish! Here are some examples of the kind of topics you could get:

teddy bears	junk	sharks
snow	picnics	bungee jumping
bananas	mosquitoes	mobile phones
Olympic Games	fishing	space travel
spiders	the bottom of the ladder	blind dates

4 Imagine you are a famous real person, dead or alive, male or female. You are aloft in a hot-air balloon basket over the Himalayas, with other famous people. The balloon begins to lose height and descends rapidly towards the snowy peaks. Some of you have to be thrown out in order for the balloon to rise again and for the rest to be saved.

Quickly decide who you are and why you are of value to the human race. One by one around the class, argue why you should stay in the basket. You have 2 minutes to justify your past, present and future existence.

Here are examples of the kind of characters you could role-play: Mozart, Mother Teresa, Shakespeare, Einstein, Elvis Presley, Pythagoras, Picasso, Ghandi, Simón Bolívar, J. K. Rowling. The teacher will decide which of you to throw out.

⑤ Desert island role play During this role play in groups of four or five, your teacher will circulate around the classroom without intervening and judge the quality of your contribution to your group discussion during each of the stages. Remember this includes listening as well as speaking skills. This project may take several lessons to complete.

> ▼ *Exam tip!*
>
> Remember that your listening as well as your speaking skills are being assessed. For a top-band mark (9 or 10) you must argue persuasively but not aggressively; act confidently as group leader; refer back to previous points; move the discussion forward; listen without interrupting; consider the views of others.

a **Stage 1**: You were on a school trip and your plane crashed on an uninhabited island. No adults survived. It is now two days later. You have explored the island and are reporting your discoveries to each other so that you can complete a map with all the resources marked on it.

Using a bigger version of the blank map on the opposite page, discuss, agree on and label the following:

     i compass point
    ii geographical features (e.g. rivers, springs, forest, cliffs, reefs) and other important places (e.g. lookout rock, beach for swimming, dangerous bog)
  iii vegetation, wildlife, food sources and hunting/fishing areas
  iv best places to build a camp and to light a signal fire
   v name for your island

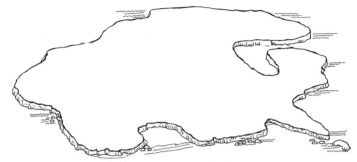

b **Stage 2**: You realise you may be on the island for some time and need a leader. Each of you should argue why you think you would or would not make a good leader. Agree on a method and select a leader.

c **Stage 3**: Several things need to be done:

- build a camp
- find a source of water
- protect yourselves from danger
- make escape or rescue possible
- ensure a regular food supply
- collect fuel for a fire

Jobs and responsibilities must be adopted by each member of the group. Discuss and decide who will do what.

d **Stage 4**: It is day 5. You realise that, unless you have some rules and punishments, people will not behave in an acceptable way or do their jobs. Discuss and agree on a list of 10 rules and on the punishments for breaking those rules.

e **Stage 5**: It is day 10 and you have become bored. To help pass the time, you agree to entertain each other around the evening campfire. After a few minutes' thought, take turns to tell a short story. (It need not be long or original. It could be an urban legend – i.e. a short horror story which is passed around orally and which people claim happened to someone they know – or the plot of a film or book, or a joke.)

f **Stage 6**: It is day 15. A dramatic incident is about to happen. Your teacher will call your group in turn to the front of the classroom, ask you to sit down and close your eyes, explain the situation you are now in, then tell you to start an improvised drama. Remember the things that have already been agreed in your group and refer to them: rules, responsibilities, island features, food supplies etc.

Here are possible scenarios:

- Someone has seen something terrifying in the trees.
- Some food has gone missing.
- There is a medical emergency.
- There is a quarrel about the leadership.
- A ship/plane has gone by because the signal fire was out.

g **Stage 7**: It is day 30. You have been rescued and are about to give a press conference back in your home town. Discuss and decide exactly how you escaped or were rescued. How do you feel about your month on the island?

Stage 8: You will not only give a press conference yourselves but also play the part of journalists to interview another group. Plan the questions and who will ask them. Ask at least one question each. Here are some questions you may wish to ask (and may need to answer), but add more of your own:

- Can you tell us exactly how you got away from the island?
- What were your main problems during the month you were there?
- Were there any casualties or illnesses during your time on the island?
- Do you think your relationships with each other have changed?
- What do you think you have learned from this experience?

Stage 9: After you have given your press conference, your teacher will give feedback on the general performance of the class during the project, say which was the best group, and award a Speaking and listening mark out of 10 to each student.

6 Your teacher will read the speech opposite. Listen to it, without reading the text yet.

7 Discuss as a class what impression the speech made on you from just listening to it. Did you notice any use of rhetoric? Which words/phrases do you remember?

8 Now look at the text. With your partner, underline the rhetorical devices of structure, vocabulary and imagery. List the underlined words/phrases and describe the device each represents. For example:

I have a dream – repetition of title

9 If you were directing this speech to be delivered in a film, what instructions would you write on the script for the actor? Discuss with your partner and annotate the text with marks and margin notes to indicate the following:

a pauses
b tone and volume changes
c pace changes
d emphasis on certain words
e body language

Dr Martin Luther King Jr addresses a crowd of 200,000 in Washington DC in 1963.

I have a dream

...I have a dream that one day on the red hills of Georgia the sons of slaves and the sons of former slaveowners will be able to sit down together at the table of brotherhood. I have a dream that one day even the state of Mississippi, sweltering with the heat of injustice, sweltering with the heat of oppression, will be transformed into an oasis of freedom and justice.

I have a dream that my four little children will one day live in a Nation where they will not be judged by the colour of their skins, but by their conduct and their character.

I have a dream that one day in Alabama, little black boys and little black girls will be able to join hands with little white boys and little white girls as brothers and sisters.

I have a dream that one day every valley shall be exalted, every hill and mountain shall be made low, the rough places will be made plane, the crooked places will be made straight.

This is our hope. This is our faith that I go back to the south with. With this faith, we will be able to hew out of the mountains of despair a stone of hope. With this faith, we will be able to transform the jangling discord of our Nation into a beautiful symphony of brotherhood. With this faith, we will be able to work together; to go to jail together; to stand up for freedom together, knowing that we will be free some day...

Martin Luther King Jr was assassinated in April 1968 by someone who did not approve of his dream.

10 Write your own *I have a dream* speech about a social, political or intellectual issue which really matters to you (e.g. animal rights, universal peace, free education for all). Make it about one and a half sides long.

Record your speech on audio- or video-tape.

Your teacher will play everyone's speech back to the class. Think about what grade you would give each speech, and why. Your teacher will award assessment grades, with references to the exam criteria.

Exam tip! See next page ▶

▼ *Exam tip!*   *relates to Exercise 10*

The first considerations when preparing a public speech are

- aim – What is the goal? (It is usually to convince, and may or may not be to entertain as well.)
- audience – Who are they, how many of them are there, and why are they there? How much do they already know? What are their expectations?
- context – How long have you got? How formal is the occasion? Is humour appropriate?

The next three aspects to be considered are

- content – Select strong points, enough but not too many; make them interesting, relevant, supported and ordered (and sometimes entertaining or original); develop each idea without spending too long on it.
- style – Use precise words, not those meant simply to impress; use devices to make you sound well informed and passionate about the issue.
- delivery – Speak more slowly than you normally would; vary pace and tone of voice; think about timing/pausing.

11 Your class is going to hold a formal debate. Your teacher will assess everyone's contribution as a speaker and listener. Follow the procedure below:

a As a class discuss and decide on a motion (subject for the debate). Your teacher writes the motion on the board in the form *This House believes that…*

b The class divides into four groups, with three to four students in each. (If the class is larger than 16 students, make six groups.) Half are told they are to speak for the motion (proposers), the other half against (opposers).

c Each group elects a speaker to deliver the group's contribution to the debate. The speaker collects and records the ideas of everyone in the group in note form. Remember, it doesn't matter whether you personally agree with the side you are presenting.

d The group selects the best points and finds support for them with examples, statistics etc. It is a good idea to try to predict the points the other side will make so that you can counteract them. The group agrees on the best order for the points.

e The elected speaker rehearses the speech quietly to his/her own group, and as a result improves it stylistically and structurally and (probably) lengthens it. Formal language is used in debate speeches, which begin *Ladies and Gentlemen…*

f The debate is conducted, with the teacher as chair, in this order: first proposer, first opposer, second proposer, second opposer etc.

g While the rest of the class – the 'floor' – listen, they are assessing the quality of the arguments and thinking of possible questions to ask when all the speeches have been delivered.

h The chair asks if there are any questions from the floor. Ask the relevant speaker for clarification of a point or challenge his/her evidence with a counter point. The speaker answers your question or challenge briefly.

i   The chair calls for votes for the motion, votes against the motion and abstentions. You vote according to the quality of the arguments and delivery, not according to your own views or friendships. Only abstain if you think both sides are equal. The teacher counts hands and announces the result of the debate.

12 Prepare and give a talk about 5 minutes long on a hobby or special interest (e.g. collecting something or belonging to a club). Your aim is to convince your audience of classmates that this is something they too would enjoy, find rewarding and should take up immediately.

Once you have prepared your talk – by planning the content, finding examples, and ordering it – practise the delivery in your head or to your partner and then perform it at the front of the class. Be prepared to answer questions at the end.

Your teacher will assess your speaking skills in this context for coursework (or the talk can be practice for the conversation task in the exam).

▼ Exam tip!

When you give a talk, your audience should be gripped from the start. Don't begin *And today I'm going to talk to you about…* . Listeners should also know when you've come to an end. Try to leave them with something to think about. You can refer discreetly to prompts but don't read from a script or cards. Make eye contact as often as possible. Don't wave your arms about or pace up and down. If you are given advance notice, visual aids can add to the effectiveness and interest of your talk.

Further practice

a   Write a self-evaluation, of about one side, of your special-interest talk after you have given it. Comment on the following:

- initial difficulties or decisions taken when planning/selecting content
- whether it went according to your expectations
- how the audience reacted
- how it compared to the talks of other students
- how you would do it differently another time

b   Listen to a political/parliamentary speech, or to extract from one, on radio or television. There are usually several on every news programme. List all the rhetorical devices you can identify, think about which ones particularly influence the listener, and judge the effectiveness of the speech/speaker.

c   Imagine an argument between two speakers: A, who strongly supports the idea of genetic engineering, and B, who is opposed to it. Script a dialogue of one and a half sides, using A and B in the margin to identify the speakers, which covers the arguments for both sides. Use emotive language and the rhetorical devices you consider most effective.

List of terms

abbreviation shortened form of a word, e.g. *Dr*

acronym word formed from the initial letters of words in a phrase, e.g. *laser (light amplification by stimulated emission of radiation)*

alliteration repetition of the initial letter in neighbouring words, e.g. *dark dank dungeon*

antithesis words balanced to create contrast

argumentative tries to convince reader that a particular attitude to something is the correct one

assonance repetition of the vowel sound in neighbouring words, e.g. *deep sleep*

autobiography account of a person's life written by him/herself

biography account of a person's life written by someone else

blurb publisher's brief description of a book printed on its back cover or jacket

brainstorm record of immediate thoughts and associations for a particular topic

chronological arrangement of events according to the time of occurrence

clause group of words containing a **finite verb**

cliché well-known and overused phrase, e.g. *Once upon a time*

climax point of greatest intensity

collate collect and combine information from two or more sources

colloquial everyday spoken language

complex sentence sentence consisting of one **main clause** and one or more **subordinate clauses**, e.g. *After he had supper, he went to bed.*

compound sentence sentence formed from two **simple sentences** using *and, but, so* or *or*, e.g. *He ate supper and he went to bed.*

connective conjunction word used to form **compound** or **complex sentences**, e.g. *but, although, since*

connotation additional implied meaning

context surrounding parts or setting of a text

descriptive tries to enable the reader to visualise something

dialogue spoken words between two or more people

direct speech speech reproduced exactly as it was spoken, in inverted commas

discursive discusses something informatively from different viewpoints

editorial newspaper or magazine editor's published comment on a topical issue

euphemism tactful or evasive way of referring to something controversial or distasteful, e.g. *passed away, ethnic cleansing*

evoke call up a response

explicit stated clearly and definitely

finite verb verb which can stand alone as the only verb in a sentence, and is not a participle

genre category of speech or writing, e.g. **narrative**

gist main ideas contained in a passage or speech

imagery pictures created in words: see **simile** or **metaphor**

imaginative see **descriptive** and **narrative**

implicit implied though not plainly expressed

inference meaning implied but not stated within a passage or speech

informative see **discursive**

logo sign representing an organisation

main clause principal clause of a **complex sentence**, which can be a sentence in its own right, e.g. *After he had supper, he went to bed.*

metaphor comparison without using *as* or *like* which uses one or more words in a non-literal way, e.g. *The ship ploughed through the waves.*

mnemonic technique for remembering something

monologue speech by one person

narrative tells a story

non-fiction believed to be true

nuance delicate difference in meaning

obituary summary of somebody's life published upon his/her death

onomatopoeia word imitating a sound

paraphrase express the same thing differently

parenthesis grammatically non-essential part of a sentence, indicated by a pair of punctuation marks

personification describing things as if they were people

phrase group of words which does not contain a **finite verb**, e.g. *behind the fountain*

plagiarism stealing the writing or ideas of another and presenting them as one's own

plot main events in a **narrative**

prefix letter or group of letters added to the beginning of a word to make a new word, e.g. *unhappy*

propaganda text which attempts to persuade others to adopt a particular political or religious viewpoint

register form of language or **genre** of expression, e.g. *colloquial, scientific*

reported speech speech which is reproduced indirectly, without inverted commas

rhetoric language features designed to persuade

scan reading of text to identify specific information

simile comparison using *as* or *like*, e.g. *She was like a fish out of water.*

simple sentence sentence consisting of a single **main clause**, e.g. *He went to bed.*

skim quick reading of a text to grasp its **gist**

spider diagram way of organising ideas as a diagram with 'legs' attached to a central 'body'

standard English widely accepted form of English, without regional variations of grammar, which can be understood by all users of the language.

structure order and organisation of content

subordinate clause clause of a **complex sentence**, generally introduced by a **connective**, which cannot stand as a sentence on its own, e.g. *After he had supper, he went to bed.*

summarise reduce a text to its essential ideas

synonym word/phrase with the same meaning as another, e.g. *try = attempt*

tension feeling of excitement or suspense

Acknowledgements

Every effort has been made to reach copyright holders. The publishers would be pleased to hear from anyone whose rights they have unwittingly infringed.

The publisher has endeavoured to ensure that the URLs for external websites referred to in this book are correct and active at the time of going to press. However, the publisher has no responsibility for the websites and can make no guarantee that a site will remain live or that the content is or will remain appropriate.

We would like to thank the following for permission to use their material in either the original or adapted form:

'Itsy bitsy spider … French "spiderman" climbs Paris skyscraper' produced by permission of ABCNEWS.com

'What's an Amish wedding like?' reproduced by kind permission of Action Video Inc.

'Indian police release pictures of Monkey Man killer' © Ananova Ltd 2002. Reproduced by permission. All rights reserved.

'Cartoonist Charles Schulz dies at 77' used with permission of The Associated Press. Copyright © 2000. All rights reserved.

'Penguins wear jumpers' reproduced by kind permission of BBC News online (www.news.bbc.co.uk).

'Day 56 – Luxor' from *Pole to Pole* by Michael Palin reproduced with the permission of BBC Worldwide Limited. Copyright © Michael Palin 1995.

'One man and his sub' © Nicholas Brautlecht by permission of the author.

The British Red Cross has granted permission to use the red cross emblem and their name on the sample letter on page 91. The Red Cross emblem is an international sign of neutral protection during armed conflicts and its use is restricted by law.

Extract from *My Family and Other Animals* by Gerald Durrell, London: Penguin, 1999. Reproduced with permission of Curtis Brown Group Ltd, London, on behalf of Gerald Durrell. Copyright © Gerald Durrell 1956.

'It's "make your mind up" time', reprinted by kind permission of *Cyprus Mail*.

'Internet teenage future global leader', 'Nicotine addiction can start after the first few cigarettes', 'Sharks', 'Land of the spirit and the Incas' reproduced by kind permission of *Cyprus Weekly*.

'Roald Dahl' © David Higham Associates Limited.

Extract from *A Sound of Thunder* by Ray Bradbury, *Colliers Magazine*, vol. 13 no. 10, October 1952. Reprinted by permission of Don Congdon Associates Inc. © 1952 by Crowell Collier Publishing, renewed by Ray Bradbury.

The Duke of Edinburgh's Award for permission to reproduce material.

'Group of Giganotosaurus found' and 'Giganotosaurus' © EnchantedLearning.com. Used by permission.

'The joys of jogging' by Emily Wilson © *The Guardian*, 12 September 2000.

'There's more to a pair of jeans' by Fran Abrams © *The Guardian*, G2, 29 May 2001.

'Culture shock of new campus life' by Jane Pearson reprinted from *The Guardian Weekly*, 13 April 2000 by permission of the author.

'Stopping by Woods on a Snowy Evening' from *The Poetry of Robert Frost,* edited by Edward Connery Lathem, copyright 1923, © 1969 by Henry Holt and Company, copyright by Robert Frost. Reprinted by permission of Henry Holt and Company, LLC.

'Clouds' from *The Times Educational Supplement*, 15 June 2001. Used by kind permission of the author, Harvey McGavin.

'The big chill' (Walter Ellis) in *The Sunday Times*, 'A rock and a hard place' (Peter and Leni Gillman) in *The Sunday Times*, 'Rescuers find trapped student cavers alive' (Charles Bremner) in *The Times*, 'The sixth sense' (Kate Rew) in *The Sunday Times*, 'Safe landing' in *The Times*, 'Rescuers find trapped student cavers alive' (Charles Bremner) in *The Times*, 'His life was cloaked in legend and myth' (Simon Sebag Montefiore) in *The Sunday Times*, 'From Russia with luck' (Caroline Gascoigne) in *The Sunday Times*, 'Scientists prove that we make our own luck' (Simon Trump and Tom Robbins) in *The Sunday Times* © NI Syndication Ltd 19 November 2000, 3 December 1995, 19 May 2001, 22 April 2001, 12 March 2000, 27 August 2001, 3 June 2001, 17 June 2001 respectively.

'The outer person is not...' by John Collee © *The Observer*, 10 December 1990.

Extract from *As I Walked Out One Midsummer Morning* by Laurie Lee © Penguin: London, 1969. Reprinted by permission of PFD on behalf of the Estate of Laurie Lee.

Extract from *The Road from Coorain: an Australian Memoir* by Jill Ker Conway, 1989, published by William Heinemann Ltd. Reprinted by permission of The Random House Group Ltd.

'Berliners flock to sample true "blind" date' in *Cyprus Review* 13 March 2001, '"Monkey Man" sows panic in India's Rajasthan' in *Cyprus Review* 25 May 2001, '"Jurassic Park" unearthed in Argentina' in *Cyprus Review* 23 February 2001 © 2001 Reuters Limited.

'Cape Town' reproduced by kind permission of SA-Venues.com

Extract from *The Wasteland* reprinted with the permission of Scribner, an imprint of Simon & Schuster Adult Publishing Group, from *Tales from a Troubled Land* by Alan Paton. Copyright © 1961 by Alan Paton; copyright renewed ©1989 by Anne Paton.

Extract from *The Woman in Black* by Susan Hill (copyright © Susan Hill, 1983) is reproduced by permission of Sheil Land Associates Ltd on behalf of Susan Hill.

'Can it be right that 400 boxing fans are paying £6 each to watch a schoolgirl fight?' from *The Daily Mail*, 19 April 2001 © Solo Syndication Ltd.

'Navel of the universe' from *The Incas and Their Ancestors: The Archaeology of Peru* by Michael E Mosley © 1992 Thames & Hudson Ltd, London. Reproduced by kind permission of Thames & Hudson Ltd, London.

Snoopy text and 'Peanuts' cartoons © United Feature Syndicate, Inc. Reproduced by permission.

Extract from *Zlata's Diary: a child's life in Sarajevo* by Zlata Filipovic, copyright © 1994 Editions Robert Laffont/Fixot. Used by permission of Viking Penguin, a division of Penguin Putnam Inc.

'I have a dream' reprinted by arrangement with the Estate of Martin Luther King Jr, c/o Writers House as agent for the proprietor, New York, N.Y. © 1963 Dr Martin Luther King Jr, copyright renewed 1991 by Coretta Scott King.

'Sharks' from *WWF News*, spring 1999 by kind permission of WWF – the global environment network.

'How to produce a good school prospectus' reproduced by kind permission of Xerox Limited.

'The Daedalus flight' © Yale-New Haven Teachers Institute from a curriculum unit, 'Daedalus: the long odyssey from myth to reality' by Anthony B. White, 1988.